WHY TEAM TEACHING?

Glenda Hanslovsky

Sue Moyer

Helen Wagner

A Charles E. Merrill Professional Book

WHY
TEAM
TEACHING?

Glenda Hanslovsky

Sue Moyer

Helen Wagner

CHARLES E. MERRILL
PUBLISHING CO.
A Bell & Howell Company
Columbus, Ohio

Standard Book Number: 675-09474-7
Library of Congress Catalog Number: 77-77138

1 2 3 4 5 6 7 8 9 10 — 75 74 73 72 71 70

Printed in the United States of America

table of contents

1 SO YOU WANT TO TEAM TEACH? 1

Definition of Terms, 3
The Teacher's Role, 7
The Administrator's Role, 10

2 GETTING UNDER WAY 13

Student Assignment to Teams, 14
Teacher Assignment to Teams, 16
Kinds of Teams, 16
Facilities and Equipment, 19

3 OPPORTUNITIES UNLIMITED 27

Program, 28
Activities for Various Group Sizes, 46
Use of Time, 47

4 RELATIONSHIPS 51

Within the Team, 52
With Other School Personnel, 59

5 CHECK-UP TIME 65

By Staff, 66
By Students, 71
By Administrators, 72

iii

By Parents, 73
By Other Teachers, 75

6   GETTING THE MESSAGE
ACROSS   77

Parents, 78
Students, 81
The Community, 81
Summary, 82

7   WHY TEAM TEACHING?   83

For the Teacher, 84
For Students, 85
For Administrators, 88
Summary, 89

BIBLIOGRAPHY   91

APPENDIX   93

Interdisciplinary Lesson Plan, 93
Interdisciplinary Assignment — I, 96
Interdisciplinary Assignment — II, 97
Interdisciplinary Assignment — III, 99
Interdisciplinary Assignment — IV, 101
Small-Group Discussion Guide, 103
Observer's Sheet, 104
Assignment Notebook Form, 105
Summary of Activities Suitable for
    Different-Sized Groups, 106
Individual Teacher's Schedule for
    One Week, 107

iv

Possible Time Usage for Students for
  One Day — A, 108
Possible Time Usage for Students for
  One Day — B, 109
Possible Time Usage for Students for
  One Day — C, 110
Weekly Schedule Plans, 111
Audio-Visual Supply Request Form, 112
Team Evaluation Form Using Open-Ended
  Sentences, 113
Team Organization on Evaluation Form, 114
Teacher Evaluation Form, 116
Open House, 117
Progress Report Form, 118
Field Trip Permit, 119

To Jules, Reed, and John

preface

What is team teaching? In today's educational ferment, the idea of team teaching crops up again and again. What's good about it? What's bad about it? Do the people who have tried it still like it? How is it different from the kind of teaching we all knew as children? How does it threaten the traditional teacher? What does it have to offer the traditional teacher? What is it trying to do? These and other questions bombard anyone interested in innovation.

This book assesses team teaching as one of many educational innovations. It can be used in many ways by readers: as a "how-to" book listing ways to prepare for and begin team teaching; as a "cookbook," with recipes to deal with the problems which inevitably face new teams; as a source of practical information based on classroom experience; as an idea center for clues on adapting a new form of teaching to old facilities, as well as to old attitudes, habits, and time and space organization. The pages to follow describe some of the demands, drawbacks, and surprises in this form of instruction. Most importantly, the book details what team teaching uniquely offers children and teachers as seen through the eyes of three experienced team teachers.

1

So You Want to Team Teach

Be not the first by whom the new are tried,
Nor yet the last to lay the old aside.

Alexander Pope

The only constant in our lives is change. New technological developments bring new opportunities, but they also bring new problems. Education is not immune to the infectious virus of change, nor to its problems. When education becomes static or a curriculum becomes *the* answer, surely the child will suffer. For as new needs are identified and new areas probed, education must move to new ways of meeting these challenges. The goal of team teaching is that of education itself: to offer each child a better chance to develop his talents and abilities.

One of today's educational innovations involves organizational patterns for teaching and learning. As one of these patterns, team teaching is gaining converts as an effective instructional method. But what is team teaching? It is many

1

things to many people. Like "permissiveness" and "individualized instruction", team teaching can mean what *you* want it to
mean. To some, it is a challenge, a challenge involving traditional disciplines or courses in education; old structures called
school houses; typical students, randomly selected; and teachers
with a wide diversity of training and background, combined to
create a program of study superior to the traditional ones.
For example, Fig. 1 illustrates a furniture arrangement which
is not traditional but is highly effective.

Figure 1. *Movable furniture permits flexible arrangements for
small group sessions; a teacher may become part of a
group or she may circulate to assist wherever she is
needed.*

The particular model or mode of team teaching is not as
important as the creative approach to it. For team teaching
can be a combination of any of the variables listed above.
Each team experience will be unique regardless of the variables,
because of the talents, abilities, and goals of the teachers and
the students involved.

Team teaching is an opportunity, an opportunity to *expand*
the talents of one teacher; to *blend* the curriculum by combin-

ing the skills of specialists, your cohorts; and to *create* new areas for exploration by students and teachers alike. But basically team teaching is a method in which a group of two or more teachers cooperate in the teaching of the same set of students. Implicit within this cooperation are both the sharing of plans and objectives for the students, and the pooling of knowledge of all sorts about the student.

Definition of Terms

Educational jargon often confuses the professional and the layman alike. For example, what do nongrading and ungrading mean to you? To argue or discuss these terms and their merit, participants must first agree on their meanings. Communication is contingent on agreement about word meanings, and this book uses terms which have come to have many meanings. For maximum clarity, definitions of terms used in this book are included here.

Team teaching, as defined above, is a technique allowing more extensive cooperation between a group of teachers working with a specified number of students. Team teaching can be much more, but it cannot be less than this bare minimum.

Team identifies the entire group of students and teachers involved together. The number of teachers and students may vary widely.

Student team alludes to all the students assigned to the group.

Team teachers is used to mean the specific teachers working with a student team.

Intradisciplinary means within a given discipline, such as an English team whose teachers offer such specialities as poetry, choral reading, and language structure. Melbourne, Florida, was a pioneer in intradisciplinary team teaching.

Interdisciplinary refers to a blending of more than one subject area. An English–social studies–science combination
represents this kind. French and art teachers working
together present another example. La Duc, Missouri,
pioneered this type of team teaching. In 1968, the entire
academic staff at East Lansing Middle School (Michigan)
was reorganized on an interdisciplinary basis.

Large group, when references are made to group sizes, indi-
cates the entire student team meeting together. An obvious
large group activity is the viewing of a film with appropriate introduction and follow-up.

Small group represents any number of children fewer than
typical classroom groupings of from twenty to thirty.
Small interest groups of six to eight, formed to pursue
ideas stimulated by a film, demonstrate one use of the
small group. Composition of a small group may be
determined informally by student choice, or formally by
teacher selection.

Independent study denotes a special kind of self-starting
activity quite different from a child sitting at a desk doing
his homework. As used here, this term refers to a voluntary and highly individual approach by a child to a subject of interest to him, and represents an additional effort
on his part unrelated to classroom demands or grades.
An example might be such projects as a group of poems,
written by a girl during a unit on the senses, or an intensive study of political cartoons culminating in student
production of original examples.

Large-group discussion means a student-participation lesson
involving the entire student team. One or more of the
team teachers may also be involved. The large group
offers a natural arena for general reaction to issues in
the news, for analysis of the content of audio-visual
presentations, and for the sharing of student concerns. A
distinction must be made between this type of activity and

total bedlam, which is the image many people have of a discussion group with one hundred students in it. Furthermore, a lecture or report is not a large-group discussion, because only one person is talking.

Small-group discussion is an ideal activity for ten or less students. Direction for the group may be formally structured, following a guide prepared either by students or teachers, with a specified goal and a time limit. On the other hand it may be an informal pursuit in which goals are dictated by the interests of the members. A teacher may or may not be a functioning member of the group.

Individualized instruction denotes provision for different levels of skill development, concept formation, and rate of learning. For instance, help is available for students who need further study in map interpretation. Students who do not need additional background aren't required to drudge through these assignments. They may work on some application of mapping of use to them, or on another lesson having nothing to do with maps at all. In addition, students with above-average verbal facility are expected to meet higher standards of excellence in oral and written work, and to demonstrate more sophisticated handling of abstractions.

In the area of concept formation, a science student might investigate the idea that all living things are interdependent. Individualized instruction enables the academically talented student to pursue this concept at the level of cause and effect, and to make hypotheses regarding its application. Meanwhile the less able individual develops his understanding of this concept with the aid of lessons carefully prepared to lead him step by step.

Individualized instruction allows for differences in rates of learning. The value of this form of teaching is especially apparent in mathematics. Students can progress through the materials at their own rate, seeking help when it is needed, and checking their progress with evaluation instruments specifically designed for various levels of achievement.

Thematic approach signifies the organization of materials and activities around broad unifying themes. This scheme borrows from many traditional units of study or from several disciplines. The theme "Life in the American Colonies" could be approached from many angles, involving such aspects as early medicine (science), land survey (math), biographies (English), and establishment of government (social studies). Fenton presents numerous examples of this and other approaches to the teaching of social studies.*

Conceptual learning differs from mere factual learning in that a basic premise rather than a sequential unit of material becomes the focal point of learning. The concept of the constancy of change, for instance, could be approached using a science focus on evolution, a social studies focus on politics, an English focus on language development, and/or a math focus on numeration systems.

The middle school is more than just a new name for a junior high. It is different. The difference in part is organizational, since middle schools often include some combination of grades five and six along with seven, eight, and nine, serving ten- to fifteen-year olds. Another difference lies in its philosophy. Middle school curricula are not watered down or abbreviated versions of high school courses of study. They are devised specifically to meet the needs of this unique age group. As Donald Eichhorn states in *The Middle School,* "To state that all youngsters in the proposed middle school are prepubescents, early adolescents or adolescents can not be justified. In reality, the transitional school contains boys and girls from all

---

*Edwin Fenton, *Teaching the New Social Studies in Secondary Schools: An Inductive Approach* (New York: Holt, Rinehart and Winston, Inc., 1966).

these designations." He goes on, "Transescence: the stage of development which begins prior to the onset of puberty and extends through the early stages of adolescence. Since puberty does not occur for all precisely at the same chronological age in human development, the transcent designation is based on the many physical, social, emotional, and intellectual changes in body chemistry that appear prior to the puberty cycle to the time in which the body gains a practical degree of stabilization over these complex pubescent changes."*

Multiage grouping involves the assignment of students to groups which cut across traditional grade lines. Groupings are based primarily on skills, interest and ability, rather than grade level. A class might consist of students from several grade levels.

Multitext approach is a system which utilizes many sources for gathering information. Rather than assignments in a single textbook, a class may use parts of eight different books to complete their studies. For instance, a class studying Nationalism might investigate the material on that topic presented in all the available texts. One source may stress the political influences, another the economic forces, and some texts might not even recognize the term. Using this approach, a student learns to compare and contrast, to communicate by sharing his information with classmates, to correlate his findings, and to recognize that no single text is the final authority.

The Teacher's Role

Teachers entering team teaching are likely to fall into one of three categories: (1) those who are employed by a school sys-

---

*Donald H. Eichhorn, *The Middle School* (New York: The Center for Applied Research in Education, Inc., 1966), p. 3.

tem which decides to adopt team teaching; (2) those who coast into this organizational system in order to facilitate schedules; or (3) those who feel there must be a more effective way to help children learn and to enable teachers to work with students and other teachers. All three categories require the individual teacher to assume the initiative in preparing to function as a member of the team. But she must do more; she must *really want* to be involved in team teaching.

The extent to which the individual teacher prepares correlates closely with the team's resulting enthusiasm, confidence, and achievement of its goals.

But how does a teacher begin to prepare? Where does she start? A popular cookbook by M. S. and C. Fitzsimmons is entitled *You Can Cook If You Can Read*. Although team teaching cannot be classified with cooking, certain skills are necessary for both, and the beginner can profit by the experience of others in both areas. So how can a teacher really get ready for team teaching?

Step 1: Read. Read everything you can get hold of about children and teaching: professional publications, and materials on curriculum, learning theories, group dynamics, behavior of children and flexible scheduling. A review of many related areas of education will help the teacher set the stage and begin to think team teaching. For truly, team teaching is not only an organizational pattern, a schedule arrangement, a time-block; it is also a "state of mind." A bibliography of suggested readings is given at the end of the book.

Step 2: Visit. Visit area schools already engaged in team teaching. If your school board can and will support such a proposal, visit more distant schools with experience in team teaching. Among these might be Lexington, Massachusetts; Ridley Township, Pennsylvania; Valley Forge Junior High, Pennsylvania; Timberlane School, New Hampshire; and C. E. MacDonald Middle School, East Lansing, Michigan. If neither of these types of visitation is plausible, find the best elementary teacher you can, and visit her classroom to observe the way she correlates ideas. Good elementary teachers have been interrelating the disciplines in their classrooms for many years. Observe how her science and social science interrelate. Note how the reading and writing activities reinforce the social studies. And, of course, music, art, speech, and craft activities afford an obvious kind of interviewing with other disciplines. For instance, we are all familiar with the use of folk music and dancing to enrich units such as world cultures.

Step 3: Look and Listen. Your administration should bring consultants to talk with teachers. These could be teachers with experience in team teaching, as well as administrators. Where this approach is impossible, write your state education association and request speakers and small group sessions at regional education meetings to explore team teaching. And then, armed with the list of questions accumulated in Steps 1 and 2, *attend* those sessions and listen to the speakers. Secure films, presenting innovations in teaching. "Make a Mighty Reach," available through the Charles Kettering Foundation, Dayton, Ohio, is such a film. Obtain the film of the CBS series "The Twenty-First Century: Education from Cradle to Classroom," on the future of education for school showing. It furnishes a glimpse into the future as it is happening right now in some schools. Now you are ready for the most critical stage of preparation.

Step 4: Dream. All teachers have said, at one time or another, "Teaching this way doesn't make sense. It would be better to. . . " If you were not limited by state requirements, standard tests, a fixed schedule as to number of periods, parental demands for students, local traditions (or ruts), what would you do? How would you teach? Why would you operate in a particular way? How would you better provide for the individual needs of students? How could your strengths be better utilized? How would you change your teaching to make it more effective for students and more challenging for you?

To find out, set up a session with interested colleagues and *brainstorm.* Most groups will find during a brainstorming session that ideas fly thick and fast. In the beginning the inclination may be to stress limitations. Familiar comments will include, "We can't do that because. . ." or ". . . but we have to have. . .," but as imagination is released, a surprising number of pragmatic possibilities evolve and you will begin to hear things like ". . . and we could also. . ." and "I'd like to. . ." Now the germ has been planted. Granted, some staff members will never welcome the idea of team teaching, or change of any type. But if you are still reading this book, you are a prime candidate for team teaching, and the opportunity to do so is a necessity for further development.

The Administrator's Role

The role of the administrator is crucial. The success of team teaching in a school depends in large part on the administrator's conviction of the value of this type of program. His responsibilities are extensive.

First, principals must be flexible enough, creative enough, and eager enough to juggle the mechanics of the organization. Schedules for teams need to be individualized to allow for maximum adaptability for all. Without the security of the traditional pattern of x number of daily periods of standard length, administrative ingenuity becomes imperative. The courage to explore endless possibilities, without being able to predict outcomes, makes possible exciting programs for teachers and students. Not all ventures will achieve the desired goals, but the right to try, and perhaps fail, is an important one. In an objective manner, principals must analyze, criticize, and evaluate failures as well as successes, because such tasks are more difficult for teachers since they are subjectively involved in the program. Close scrutiny of the program establishes guidelines for future directions in team teaching.

Second, administrators must make it possible for teachers to prepare. Additional time for teachers to pursue ideas may be secured by releasing them from busy work, by providing teacher aides, and by calling staff meetings only when absolutely necessary. By drawing on their own wisdom and experience in group dynamics, principals should encourage teachers to ask questions and express concerns, and then they should take appropriate action. Funds must be made available for setting up a professional library and for visitations and consultants.

But perhaps their single most important contribution is to provide a climate for innovation. Even the most gifted teacher can only grow professionally and creatively in that climate which permits the challenge of growth and experimentation.

Another important aspect of the administrator's role is the preparation of the community for innovations in teaching. Regardless of the merit of a new idea, it cannot possibly succeed without the positive support of the majority of the community. Change usually brings confusion and frustration. Only when positive groundwork has been laid can the inevitable crises be resolved. Parents of students in the program, and the community in general, need and deserve to understand the general basis for team teaching and its specific relationship to their children. Through parent organizations, service clubs, study groups, and news media, the administration must prepare the community for team teaching.

Although there is an unfortunate nationwide trend separating teachers and administrators at the bargaining table, they remain interdependent in their educational roles. By maintaining these complementary positions, they not only support each other, but promote the maximal educational development of their students.

The school board will depend on the administration to explain the adoption of a new program and to justify the expenditure of monies for such programs. They will want assurance of the merit of these innovations for the children of their community.

Now that the terms used in this book have been explained, and suggestions for preparation for team teaching have been given, specific procedures for actually beginning the program must be considered. Chapter 2 presents concrete ideas for the organization of teams.

2 Getting Under Way

He has half the deed done who has
made a beginning.

Horace

Once the professional group and the public are prepared for
team teaching, it is time to initiate a program. To begin, the
specifics of organization, such as team composition and facilities, must be identified.

When a team of students and teachers is to be formed, at
least three basic questions need to be answered at the administrative level: (1) What disciplines will be represented in this
team? (2) How are the students to be selected? and (3) How
are the teachers to be assigned? The same questions are pertinent when an entire school is to be teamed. With some degree
of teacher involvement, more thorough and harmonious decisions can be reached concerning these basic questions.

A team may represent a single discipline, or may be a combination of several. If more than one discipline is included in a single team, choices must be made as to how many disciplines shall be incorporated and which ones they shall be.

Some subjects traditionally have fitted together better than others, such as the familiar English-social studies and math-science blocks. But a team may wish to include all the academic areas offered by the school or some part of them. Teachers may decide that social studies, art, and vocal music can best accomplish their goals for the students. A foreign language teacher may cooperate with other disciplines, emphasizing the culture of the country whose language is being studied. Only the ingenuity and patience of the staff limit the possibilities here.

Student Assignment to Teams

Questions about student assignment to a team logically follow the choice of disciplines, but are also affected by other factors. Community desires for children and whether the school is rural, consolidated, urban, suburban, or special do much to shape school policy, including the grouping of students. Furthermore, the preferences of teachers, tradition in the community, and team objectives may indicate or even require one choice of grouping rather than another. In addition, one needs to consider the percentage of college-bound students, the percentage for whom the high school is terminal, and the value the community places upon education.

Two familiar types of grouping are homogeneous and heterogeneous. The individual school must determine for itself how it can best use these two types. It is possible to use both types of grouping within one school or within one team.

Homogeneous grouping, which involves students of similar interest, skills and abilities, may be more productive for some teams. This grouping is particularly applicable to a team embarking on an extremely rigorous experimental program requiring above-average skills of its students. A team designed to have very small classes and work with severely disadvantaged youngsters must also be restricted to this type of arrangement. Musically talented students interested in creating a production as a team project typify grouping dictated by team purpose.

Many teams may prefer heterogeneous grouping in which pupils of various skills and abilities are assigned together. Under this arrangement, the team teachers can group and regroup students depending upon the activity being pursued that day, and the purposes of a given lesson.

Random selection, however, is not the same thing as heterogeneous grouping. To be truly random, such selection implies a completely neutral drawing of names from the school roll, without any kind of screening. Teams chosen in this manner may include students who speak no English, those with physical disabilities or emotional disorders, or even the mentally unstable. Such children may find the team setup offers them less security, because it is so flexible. If an entire school is being teamed, then each team can carry its share of these youngsters who require so much extra help and individual attention. On the other hand, an experimental or pilot team may wish to exclude one or more of these categories of exceptional children, to permit optimal functioning of the new venture.

Once the type of grouping is determined, the administrator should publicize it widely along with some supporting reasons for the choice. Teachers and parents who understand the groupings will more readily support them. Parents will need reassurance that any child not disruptive of a normal classroom can be a successful team member. Indeed, the child who is unusual may well find, within the larger more diverse membership of a team, a kindred spirit to bolster his ego while he learns to be more socially acceptable to a wider group. Chapter 3 discusses student interaction within a team at more length.

Teacher Assignment to Teams

Selection of teachers for teams may be accomplished in several ways. The administrator may make the decision alone or he may honor teacher requests. An administrator may wish to base team composition upon such considerations as the age, sex, and years of experience of his teachers. In this way, he can apportion the tyro and the veteran, the male and the female, the innovative and the traditional teacher among the teams. If the relevant criteria are previously discussed with the faculty, forthcoming decisions based upon them will be more readily accepted.

Many patterns of team membership can be successful. It may be possible for the interested teachers to select the members of the staff with whom they wish to work. This method has the obvious advantage of ensuring compatible staff relationships within a team. However, one danger of this system is that it may serve to strengthen staff cliques. If a team's teachers are chosen by the principal, as in many successful teams, new strengths may emerge from the interaction of teachers who had not previously worked together. Some schools prefer to change the staff of a team yearly, on the assumption that each teacher is professional enough to work with any other teacher for a year. An administrator may want to keep a particularly successful team intact, to reach for still greater achievements the following year. Contrarily, he may choose to disband it and use its members to strengthen less flourishing teams. Chapter 4 includes a discussion of relationships between teachers on the same team.

Kinds of Teams

Teams, like students and teachers, come in a variety of sizes and kinds. Selection of the type of team, however, can be influenced by levels of instruction. Although a team can be created to fill any need, the most common kinds are "special," intra- and interdisciplinary.

A familiar type we've all known is the loosely built one often occurring in elementary schools, in which two teachers trade classes several times a week for special units, so that each can teach her own strengths. Their cooperation occurs at odd moments over lunch or after school, when they compare notes and make plans together. The lack of time often limits their planning to the mechanics of scheduling.

A well-known example of intradisciplinary team teaching, often occurring in high schools, finds an entire department offering a unit designed to take advantage of teacher strengths. In an English departmental team, the students from several classes may meet in the auditorium for several lecture-discussions on poetry given by the staff member whose forte this is. Or the regular English teacher may be replaced by another who conducts the scheduled class sessions on language structure, descriptive writing, or some other related topic.

In these types of intradisciplinary teams, all science teachers or English teachers or math teachers plan together the material to which students will be exposed. Each of the teach-

Figure 2. *Hearing the viewpoints of several teachers, as well as several students, provides a broader basis from which a student can draw his own conclusions.*

ers presents an area, perhaps the area of his greatest strength
or interest, to the assigned group of students while the other
team teachers circulate, giving individual assistance as needed
(see Fig. 2). One of the other teachers assumes responsibility
for the presentation of another body of material at another
time, and so it goes. Although each lesson is the responsibility
of designated teachers, all are free to follow up in their own
way by working with small groups, seminars, and students on
independent study.

Through this method of sharing responsibility, the team is
assured of a higher quality of presentation from its teachers.
Facing a large group without adequate preparation is an experience no teacher willingly repeats. The team organization
allows for more careful planning of content and more attention to methods and visual aids.

Students benefit by exposure to the same material, which
furnishes a common basis for later discussion and evaluation.
By limiting the number of times a teacher must make the same
presentation, a maximum of enthusiasm and excitement can
be guaranteed. Every teacher has faced the problem of presenting the same material to five or six classes in succession. Not
only is it difficult for a teacher to generate the same degree of
enthusiasm for each presentation, but each class also receives a
slightly different interpretation. Sometimes critical material is
inadvertently omitted.

In an interdisciplinary organizational pattern, the team is
comprised of teachers from *several* disciplines, e.g., math, science, social studies, and English. This team might be assigned
a block of time and a fixed number of students. The goals of
such a group would be to combine the teachings of the various
disciplines with flexible use of time, facilities, and group sizes
as needed. As one becomes more involved and more experienced, the opportunities and the possibilities become broader.
The blending of disciplines becomes such a logical way of
teaching and learning that one wonders why this system took
so long to be generally accepted. Chapter 3 on program discusses such blendings in greater detail.

Using the "school within a school" idea, special area teachers can also be assigned to a team to complete the student's schedule. Such a grouping enables teachers of art, music, and speech to blend their activities with those of the academic areas without sacrificing the specific skill development and cultural experiences their disciplines offer.

Regardless of the kind of team, assignment of a counselor to meet regularly with its teachers is a good idea. Greater understanding of students results when teachers and counselors exchange nonconfidential information about individual differences and concerns. Discussion about students and their problems occupies a large percentage of team planning time. The assistance of a trained counselor can strengthen the total team efforts in behalf of the students. The counselor's technical knowledge is invaluable to the classroom teacher in her handling of exceptional students.

Facilities and Equipment

One of the natural concerns of a team is the space available for its activities. Most teams will occupy old buildings, which are less than ideal for team teaching. The lack of flexibility in such structures may deter the novice or offer a ready excuse to the administrator not fully committed to this innovation. Yet teachers *can* and *do* team teach in old buildings, overcoming by their own flexibility the rigidity inherent in their boxes-within-a-box. It's hard, of course, but it's possible. Although flexible facilities are a must for maximum effectiveness, teams can operate well enough in traditional buildings to taste the invigorating wine of success.

As long as the facilities include a room large enough to accommodate the entire team with writing surfaces, team teaching can become a reality. In older buildings an auditorium can be adapted to this purpose. Lapboards can be used effectively if armdesks are not available. Sometimes the cafeteria affords such a meeting room. If the gym is free while physical education classes are using outdoor areas, its spaciousness offers an ideal place for total team sessions such as movies. A valuable use of these large group areas permits students to work in numerous "isolated" small discussion groups before reassembling for a total group sharing of ideas and a wrap-up. Several conceivable arrangements are suggested in Figs. 3-6.

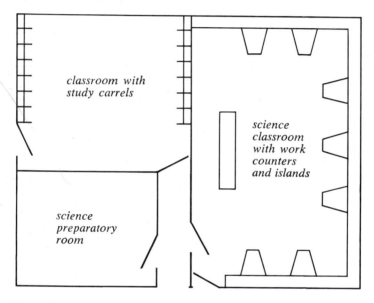

Figure 3. *Cluster of two classrooms.*

Many newer buildings contain areas separated by folding or sliding doors instead of permanent walls. Such arrangements permit great flexibility with minimal time spent in rearranging groups. Perhaps the ideal accommodation would consist of clusters, a group of three or more classrooms separated by sliding doors, which may be opened to permit seating of the entire team. The cluster should have enough separate rooms to accommodate the entire team in standard class-size groups of twenty to thirty students, in a variety of activities.

Ideally, the team meeting rooms should be convenient to the learning center, or library. Opportunity can thus be provided for students to work independently in the learning center while the team teachers work with other groups in the classroom.

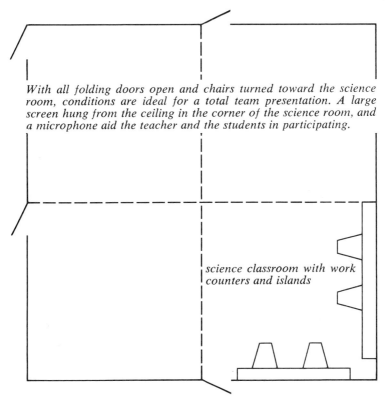

With all folding doors open and chairs turned toward the science room, conditions are ideal for a total team presentation. A large screen hung from the ceiling in the corner of the science room, and a microphone aid the teacher and the students in participating.

science classroom with work counters and islands

Figure 4. *Cluster of four classrooms.*

This facility, the learning center, may contain small conference rooms, centers for specialized activity, and possibly even a classroom area. The teacher trying to meet individual needs can utilize these various areas as she desires. A group of five or six students planning a debate may meet in a conference room.

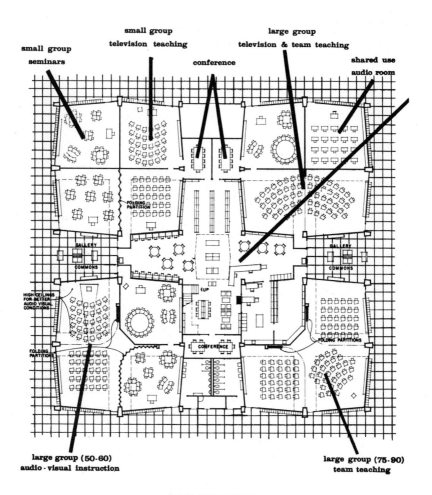

small group
seminars

small group
television teaching

large group
television & team teaching

conference

shared use
audio room

large group (50-60)
audio - visual instruction

large group (75-90)
team teaching

FIRST FLOOR PLAN

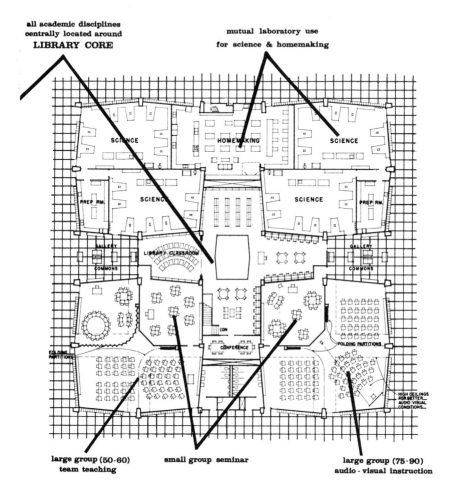

all academic disciplines
centrally located around
LIBRARY CORE

mutual laboratory use
for science & homemaking

large group (50-60)
team teaching

small group seminar

large group (75-90)
audio - visual instruction

SECOND FLOOR PLAN

Figure 5. *This entire building was designed to allow maximum flexibility in a team teaching program. Academic classrooms are located together, permitting interrelationship of subject matter. Because of its location, the learning center serves as the dynamic core for the entire building.*

Courtesy of Warren Holmes Co., Architects.

An individual preparing a time line or a map would find enough space to amass, spread out, and use the many sources he needed. Without disturbing others, students can use earphones to preview a filmstrip with an accompanying record. The library classroom is ideal for orientation of students to this facility. It is easier for students to learn the location of specific materials when surrounded by them.

In any school, one of the most versatile facilities for independent work is the study carrel. This individual study booth can be equipped for use with filmstrip viewers, tape recorders, and record players with earphones, or it may simply be a place for study. Because they block visual stimuli, study carrels are more conducive to concentration. Their compactness allows their placement in many different locations: classrooms, libraries, and even in hallways.

Figure 6. *Within a cluster of rooms, several activities may be occurring at the same time; here, one group listens to a teacher while another works on individual activities and a third group concentrates on material written on the chalkboard.*

Since some activities will involve the total group, availability of audio-visual equipment must be assured. The overhead projector should be standard room equipment, because chalkboards for a large group are ineffectual. Transparencies for the overhead projector can be used in a variety of ways as effective teaching aids. Use of the overhead for some scientific demonstrations enables all students simultaneously to see clearly such things as energy waves in water and polarized light. The math teacher will use the overhead for exercises involving plotting graphs on transparent grids and for demonstrating problem-solving techniques. The use of colored overlays for teaching social studies vividly recreates historical events and territorial acquisitions. Projection of transparencies of an actual student composition on an overhead gives new meaning to the need for clear expression. Transparencies permit the teacher to write directly on the copy and then erase the writing so the overlay may be reused.

As in standard classrooms, movie, filmstrip, and slide projectors are needed. In addition, individual viewers for slides and filmstrips enable students to make up work, to review, and to study in depth and at their own pace. By adding study carrels to the classroom, much of this equipment can be used by individuals without disturbing the rest of the class. A tape recorder, while often considered a luxury, is almost a necessity for a large team operation. When lectures, guest speakers, or student presentations are offered to the total group, they can be taped. Not only can this tape be used by those who were absent, but its availability for review by any student is extremely valuable.

For reinforcement and enrichment, a record player is desirable. Increasingly, recordings are being made available to accompany themes, units, and individual studies of a given subject. They are a worthwhile adjunct to many current filmstrips.

Although experienced teachers can probably project their voices to the group, a microphone arrangement is needed for student and guest use. A portable, battery-operated microphone hook-up is especially desirable because it allows the teacher to move about freely. If you have a tape recorder, its microphone can be used.

Large movable bulletin boards and chalkboards are convenient. Materials assembled on these can be shuttled between study and teaching stations as needed. Furniture in all team rooms should be movable, allowing for groups of different sizes and tasks of different kinds. While other movable furniture is a convenience for team teaching, movable book carts are a necessity. They afford greater ease in transporting heavy supplies quickly from station to station, as required by the frequent changes in size, composition, and purpose of student groups. The idea of a room-set of books is antiquated in team teaching.

Since the collection and distribution of papers becomes more complicated with a larger, more flexible group, some ingenuity will be required to simplify this problem. One solution might be collection and distribution according to numbers assigned to students. One group solved this problem with the construction of numerous labeled compartments, alphabetically arranged. Teacher aides placed papers to be returned in the proper compartments and the student, at his convenience, retrieved his own materials.

A good maxim when a problem seems overwhelming is simply to ask the students for suggestions for its solution. One hundred youngsters can produce more solutions than a teacher could dream up in a year.

3   Opportunities Unlimited

A day to fire the brave,
And warm the cold,
To gain new glories,
Or augment the old.

Alexander Pope

Team teaching offers unlimited opportunities in many areas: ways of approaching and relating subject matter, techniques for helping individual students meet their varying needs, arrangements of groups according to objectives, and activities appropriate to groups of different size and periods of different length. Opportunities are greater in team teaching because the necessary ingredients for flexibility are inherent. The scheduling of teachers with time and students in common is the crucial factor differentiating this organizational pattern from the traditional classroom.

27

Program

If team teaching offers opportunities unlimited, how does curriculum serve as a guide without hindering innovation? In the interdisciplinary approach to team teaching, curriculum provides the fabric upon which different disciplines using different colored threads weave their kaleidoscope of color into a tapestry. The pattern and the texture of this tapestry will be influenced by the varying structures of the disciplines involved. If four academic areas, such as mathematics, English, social studies, and science are included in one team, the pattern of their interweaving will be quite different from that of a team which includes only three of these areas, or some other combination of disciplines.

Interweaving will be limited if each discipline is bound to its own traditional course of study. Except for occasional opportunities, a prearranged program organized solely by departments will not lend itself to interdisciplinary blendings.

What, then is conducive to the exciting exchange which is part of team teaching? Enthusiastic and well-trained teachers, the rich largess of electives, and the flexibility of disciplines contribute to the total picture. The value of the first two is obvious; the third is not so obvious but can be clarified by the following example. If a unit on the senses is being studied in English, science classes could be studying tools with which man extends his senses (microscopes, telescopes, stereo, cameras, etc.). At the same time, math classes might pursue the measurement of information gained through our senses, such as graphing and statistical analysis. The social studies classes might examine the importance of man's awareness of others gained through use of his "sharpened" senses.

Another approach is the use of one discipline as the focus or hub of a lesson, with the other subject areas playing a supportive role. Certain disciplines are more adaptable than others for this purpose.

Social studies, for example, is particularly well-suited for interdisciplinary team teaching, if the material is not approached chronologically. In a unit on the Civil War, while social studies emphasizes the economic, political, and social causes contributing to the war, science supplements by studying health and medical conditions of this time. English enriches the study by investigating the vast amounts of literature written about this crisis including not only short stories, novels, and biographies, but also journals. Composition assignments could be based on observation and keeping a journal. A cooperating mathematics teacher bases his assignments on Civil War data such as statistics of casualties, enlistments, and distances traveled between major battles. These lessons would involve computational skills, the use of various measurements, charting and graphing techniques, and the creation and interpretation of story problems.

Any restrictive patterning of one discipline fragments other team disciplines, and makes interrelating more difficult. As stated above, the strict chronological approach to social studies limits its versatility as a focus. Likewise, mathematics, when taught only sequentially as required by many courses of study, is rigid and less adaptable as the core discipline.

No team of teachers can consistently find meaningful correlations or well-integrated units. However, with experience the way to use any discipline as a focus becomes more readily apparent. Contrived blendings of subject matter can then be avoided, and when the interrelationship is obvious and strong, exciting concepts can be pursued. As a result, the cohesiveness of the disciplines becomes the natural order.

The following lesson typifies interrelationships between English, science, and social studies, with the help of a teacher familiar with principles of art. When the public library in our town secured a set of enlarged photographs from the book *The Family of Man*, the authors decided to use the display for a lesson. The library was only a block from the school, and all the students could visit it during their lunch hour, after school, or during the evening.

As an introduction, the social studies teacher led a large-group discussion designed to determine what experiences and needs were common to people of every culture, around the world. Students came up with love and family, work and play, learning, friends, and the satisfaction of physical needs.

Following this discussion, the science teacher displayed a large colored travel poster of Rome's Spanish Steps. The students were asked their reactions to the picture, and then pressed for the reasons why they reacted as they did. In the process they discovered the built-in allure the photographer had captured: bright blue sky, many colors, gaily dressed people, and busy content of scene.

At this point the art teacher gave some tips on technical composition, pointing out how the photographer had placed his people slightly off center, and dwarfed by the stones, but spotlighted by a shaft of bright sunlight. Line, texture, and contrast were explained and demonstrated. Similarly, she showed how light and dark were used in a black-and-white poster to do all that color had done in the first one. Finally, the students were asked to squint their eyes to look for the focus and design in each poster.

Each student then received a copy of the following assignment.

SPECIAL ASSIGNMENT FOR A TEAM

A few years ago, a group of outstanding photographers compiled a series of pictures into a book called *The Family of Man.* These candid pictures, taken of people of every race, portray the common threads which bind together the peoples of all nations: work, play, the search for a better life, learning, family and friends, and the greatest bond of all, love.

Some of those photographs are now on display in the public library in the south hall. Some time before Thursday morning, look at these pictures and find one you especially like. Take notes on whatever it is about the pictures that speaks to you: its characters, theme, lighting, contrast, use of symbols, the attitudes of the people in it, etc. On Thursday in class you will be given an opportunity to discuss: (1) the picture you chose, (2) what helped you form an opinion of the character of the person in the picture, and (3) how the camera emphasized these parts.

On Thursday, after some preliminary large-group discussion designed to be a warm-up, each child was asked to write about "his" picture. After identifying it, each told why it was his choice, and added a paragraph on the techniques used by the cameraman to secure such a striking effect. In the process, he used all the English skills at his command: word usage, sentence and paragraph construction, use of vivid modifiers, and punctuation. The finished product was graded once by the English teacher, looking for just these skills, and once by the science teacher on the analysis of the photographic methods involved. (Refer to the Appendix for other examples of interdisciplinary team teaching.)

Another way of approaching subject areas is through the cooperation of teachers within a given discipline. One high school social studies department capitalized upon unique teacher strengths in an introductory course comprised of anthropology, sociology, psychology, and economics. Each staff member took responsibility for that section of the program for which he was best prepared. (For more information about intradisciplinary team teaching, see Chapter 2, "Kinds of Teams.")

A third kind of team teaching is special because it is designed to fulfill one specific purpose. During a school year, an expert putting in a single appearance can embellish basic learnings. Such an expert could be any staff member, parent, or community resource person. This type of special lesson extends the students' understandings, demonstrates broader applications of facts in hand, and makes learning more exciting. The use of an outside person differs from the usual use of a guest speaker in that the offering is designed to reach specific prearranged objectives.

A middle school team focused one day's activities upon the flag; its traditions, its history, its care and handling, and the music associated with it. In this example of a special team, students assumed unusual leadership roles. A group of Boy Scouts demonstrated a Color Guard ceremony, followed by proper flag etiquette. Several other students presented a skit depicting the construction of the first U. S. Flag. The social studies teacher discussed the conditions under which Francis Scott Key wrote the words to the "Star Spangled Banner" during the War of 1812. The English teacher with the aid of overhead transparencies analyzed the precise language used by Key to reveal his emotions. In a musical climax to the program, the choir instructor traced the progression of the melody of "The Star Spangled Banner" and accompanied the team in group singing.

As in any good classroom, a team classroom requires a variety of techniques for meeting the needs of individual students. All students share the need to become increasingly independent, to make friends and become socially acceptable, and to learn how to study. Additional needs of students operating in teams include the need to function effectively in a large group, the need to benefit from small group membership, the need for remedial assistance, and the opportunity for certain students for independent study.

Techniques for meeting these needs vary with the teacher. One of the conditions most misunderstood by parents, students, and teachers is the large-group participation lesson. Parents often feel their child will be lost in the large group. Students fear such a large audience. And teachers dread maintaining discipline for so many.

Surprisingly, some teams have found discipline to be less of a problem in the large group, once steps were taken to enlist student cooperation. It helps to remember that the large group *can* be used effectively for discussion, and not only for such obviously suitable activities as tests, guest speakers, and audio-visual presentations (see Fig. 7). A good way to begin is to take the steps mentioned above the very first day. For example, after a discussion of the size of the student team and personal freedom, ask the students what conditions are necessary for optimal team functioning. The sincerity, fairness, and maturity of their replies will be an eye-opener. Pursuing ideas for team cooperation is conducive to a free large-group discussion because every student has a personal interest, yet each is free from the pressure of grades or of recall of factual information. During the next team sessions, encourage students to ask questions, discuss their school problems or concerns, and share with others general orientation information. From these informal discussions, and the ability to handle subjects of this nature, there is a gradual transfer of the skills necessary for large-group discussion of academic concerns.

Figure 7. *Placement of a large screen in one corner of a three- or four-room cluster enables a large group to see a film together.*

A few tips on handling the large group may be in order here:

(1) In your anxiety to have things "move" in the large group, be aware of the handful who will want to carry the discussion and answer all the questions.

(2) Put the troublemakers in exposed places and maintain frequent eye contact.

(3) Keep a large group a shorter time.

(4) Make use of any audio-visual materials and equipment including a microphone which you need to make you more effective.

(5) Use the Socratic method of questioning when they least expect it.

(6) Make liberal use of the discovery technique of learning.

(7) Change your location while you teach.

(8) Have the whole team wear name tags the first few weeks.

(9) Prepare, post, and use seating charts.

(10) Establish a definite routine for large-group sessions.

(11) Begin at the scheduled time, and penalize latecomers.

(12) Devise a workable system for doing the "household" chores, such as taking attendance, collecting, and returning papers. Large boxes with appropriate labels for students to deposit papers in may help with this chore.

(13) Establish a team communication system.
  (a) Post the day's date.
  (b) Arrange shortcuts for informing students about recurring details. A red piece of construction paper on the bulletin board may remind all students to bring science notebooks to class. Other signals may indicate the need for wearing coats for a field trip, a room change, a schedule change, etc.
  (c) Designate a special bulletin board space for school announcements important to all students.
  (d) Distribute printed instructions whenever possible.

Another large-group skill all students need to perfect is to learn to listen to the questions and opinions of others. A counselor can serve as a valuable adjunct to the student team by discussing with its members the responsibilities of the individual to the group. Careful reinforcement of these courtesies before and after group sessions is a worthwhile technique. Team teachers, too, need to honor these fundamentals of group interaction, if they expect to provide a climate for the free and cooperative exchange of ideas. A student may gain additional confidence from the thought that in a large group, there is bound to be someone who feels as he does.

The fastest way to undo the positive group climate and to create discipline problems is to resort to extensive or frequent lectures. Contrarily, one of the most exciting experiences of team teaching is to see a group of students enthusiastically pursuing a controversial subject in a large-group discussion.

The field trip, another large-group activity, can be a marvelous aid to learning or it can be a complete fiasco and waste of time. A successful field trip has more worth than just the trip itself. Students must understand the purpose of such a trip and how it relates to their classroom activities. They should be instructed to make specific observations, to note exact dates and occurrences, and to record definite information. Upon return to the classroom, follow-up discussions, written activities, or summarizations based on their observations will make the field trip the valuable aid to learning that it should be.

If possible, the teacher should visit the site before taking her class. Thus, she can decide which areas offer greatest support for her classroom activities, and she can become acquainted with the people in charge and their requirements for students (no chewing gum, no admittance to certain exhibits unless accompanied by designated personnel, no picking of flowers along nature trails, etc.). But most important, she can sketch a map of the area to be visited if none is available. All of us have seen children wandering aimlessly from room to room and floor to floor of museums, seeing little and remembering less, until they arrive at the sales counter. A map with starred items of particular importance will enable students and their supervisors to look and learn with a minimum of wasted time.

The following brief article, "How to Survive a Field Trip"* offers serio-comic suggestions which all teachers can enjoy.

1. Make sure your field trip has a purpose.

2. Preview each trip personally. Be suspicious of all promotional folders. Find out for yourself where the rest rooms, eating facilities, and on-duty nurses are.

3. Make trip reservations well in advance. Insist on a confirming letter and carry it with you. To avoid crowds, go on your trip during the off season.

4. Prepare the children for the trip. If possible, arrange for a guide.

5. See that an adult is with each group of children throughout the trip. Reliable parents are a must. Janey's mother may be a whiz at flower arranging, but how will she hold up on a field trip? Don't guess; know!

6. Wear comfortable shoes.

7. Keep your group to a manageable size.

8. Assign partners; two children are always easier to find than one. Select a place to meet if you get lost. Above all, don't panic. Someone is bound to realize that the teacher is missing before it's time to board the bus.

9. Carry a first-aid kit, a cache of plastic bags for children who get carsick, and the usual supply of aspirin and spirits of ammonia for yourself.

10. Never send a child into a public rest room alone. Send boys in groups of four. If any unusual sounds, such as absolute quiet, persist beyond 30 seconds, feel free to investigate.

11. When children are going to eat lunch on the bus, take along a carton for waste disposal. Forbid bottled drinks— broken glass is messy—and carry a can opener.

---

*Gene McMillan and Evelyn Stryker, "How to Survive a Field Trip," *NEA Journal* (October, 1967), p. 58.

12. Always pack an extra peanut butter and jelly sandwich for the child who thinks the Great Swamp is a drive-in where he can buy his lunch.

13. Mince no words about trip behavior. Have simple rules and stick to them. Also make it clear that you will not be responsible for carrying cameras, changing film, returning unchewed bubble gum, or locating lost comic books, sweaters, and baseball cards.

14. Pick a reliable bus company. Losing a wheel on the turnpike makes great conversation but may create problems.

15. Keep a list of all children who are on the trip and count noses constantly. You might find a count-off system helpful.

16. Tattoo the school phone number on your wrist for emergency use. The principal likes to have something to tell parents if you're three hours late.

17. If the trip is to extend beyond the regular school day, set a time for parents to pick up their children.

18. Keep smiling. Tomorrow you can spend the whole day teaching.

Participating in a small group would seem to be a simple task for an individual, but many students need help in learning to function easily in this setup. Some students are uncomfortable with the exposure a small group affords, and are reluctant to face the reactions of other members. As opposed to his feeling of security in the large group, a student in a small group may feel conspicuous. There is no comforting anonymity in the small group as there is in the large.

One of the easiest ways to facilitate a student's participation is to structure the session by assigning a definite topic or question to be pursued. The teacher may help further by appointing specific members to serve in the designated roles of leader, recorder, and observer. An additional student may be chosen to report the group's findings to the team. (See Appendix, "Small-Group Discussion Guide" and "Observer's Sheet.") It is the duty of the teacher during these early sessions to insure the rotation of roles within the group. Very soon the students will eagerly assume the responsibility for the operation of their own groups. A wise teacher will form groups representing a cross section of the student team, in order to provide for group interaction at all levels. The development of empathy for fellow human beings, begun in the large group, is continued in small groups, as each member makes his contribution. The opportunity to assess the ideas of others, and to submit his own ideas for evaluation, greatly encourages individual growth and development.

Introducing material to the student team, then dividing into small groups to pursue the ideas in depth, then reassembling the total group epitomize the flexibility of team organization. To obtain the maximum benefits for the students from this flexibility, a teacher needs to help them polish both small- and large-group skills.

The availability of more than one teacher in a team offers the advantage of tutorial assistance for students requiring remedial help (see Figs. 8-9). Since this need can come upon any student at some time during the year, a team's teachers can provide a special open lab time for meeting it. During this time, all team students are scheduled to be with their homeroom team teacher. However, after appearing for roll check, each can decide for himself what is the best use of this open lab time (see Fig. 10).

There are at least as many choices as there are team teachers. If the student needs to see any of them about a missed assignment, to make up a test, for help with some work he does not understand, or just to use texts or materials in that teacher's room, he signs out to go there. A student just back after an absence may need to visit all his team teachers in turn. Some students may choose to go to the library to complete an assignment requiring the use of filmstrips and records. Students on independent study will have all the facilities of the school available during this time, as well as an opportunity to discuss their projects with the team teacher in whose area they are probing. Finally, any child can use the open lab time to work on assignments, study for a test, get notes from a friend, read for enjoyment, or finish up a lab or some classwork.

It should be apparent from these examples that open lab is as different from study hall as independent study is from doing

Figure 8. *While other team teachers work with the bulk of the team, one teacher is free to work with individual students.*

homework. Scheduling such a short period of work on a regular or semiregular basis several times a week will be a boon to students. It will also do away with the horrible rush at the beginning and end of class periods when frantic students try to get help from teachers who are also trying to conduct a class. If an entire school is team teaching, it may well be possible for an administrator so to schedule his teams that more than just the team teachers would be available for consultation during this open lab time.

Encouraging students to attempt independent study requires the teacher to use special methods. As defined in Chapter 1, independent study presupposes initiative, curiosity, and enough

Figure 9. *When folding doors between rooms are opened, one teacher can supervise several groups at once. This frees other team teachers to help with individual needs of students.*

self-discipline on the part of the student to work alone on a subject, unaffected by the usual classroom demands. Not every child has the interest or the skills to pursue independent study. Not every child can do the required school work, with adequate time to explore additional areas. Extensive out-of-school interests and responsibilities preclude independent study endeavors for some students. Others must concentrate fully in order to master basic reading and writing skills, and would view independent study as an impossible load.

Which students *can* be involved in independent study? The four basic types are: students who are well-organized; students who reveal self-direction in exploring an interest; students who have adequate basic skills, and those who show above-average academic performance or unusual maturity. A student may well fit into more than one of these categories.

The special teacher techniques for promoting independent study include *inspiring* the students to go beyond the minimum, *encouraging* their curiosity, *providing* materials, *stimulating* their interests, and *assisting* students to select and delimit a manageable piece of work. Never underestimate the value of

Figure 10. *Some students choose to use their open lab time to further an interest in science.*

exhibiting interest in them and their pursuits, listening to them, and being aware of their interests and talents. Usually it is wise for teachers to schedule time for checking daily progress of students on independent study, and to provide for frequent student self-evaluation.

The variety of independent projects is endless. A student may choose to do outside reading about a particularly colorful historical figure, or demonstrate a ham radio during a class unit on electricity. Other choices may include working through a book of math puzzles for sheer enjoyment, doing a comparative study of African and American dances, or reporting on archaeological findings about early man, arising from a study of contemporary African civilizations.

The range of possible independent study activities in a team setup is limited only by the ingenuity of the team members involved. Given the opportunity, a student may take the group on a trip through a natural history museum, on around-the-world flights, into battle with war heroes, diving in a submarine, to a coffee klatsch with Harpo Marx, folk-singing, and far deeper into subjects of interest to him than an adult might deem possible. Students may write tales of imaginary "warriors" battling smallpox, the Redcoats, and the winter of 1777-78 at Valley Forge. They may become fighters of yellow fever, a co-worker of Albert Schweitzer, or George Washington's chief counsel at Trenton as they parlay the results of independent study into presentations for the team.

Closely allied to the development of independent study skills is the teacher objective of helping each student to assume as much independence and responsibility as he can handle. A teacher can ask for no greater achievement for her student during the year than to see evidence of growth in these two areas, because they strongly influence student happiness and success. There is no quick or easy way to develop these traits; however, possibilities for unlimited flexibility inherent within the team approach facilitate the pursuit of these two major goals for each student. Consistent and concerted effort by both teacher and student are required if growth is to occur. Many facets contribute to the development of these skills. The teacher can help by providing (1) certain specific activities designed to polish skills, (2) opportunities to practice, and (3) appreciation of student efforts to exhibit them.

Since "organization" seems to be one of the major problems of students, much stress must be placed on helping students "organize" their time, their procedures, and their materials. Each student should have a list of supplies to bring to class every day in order to function effectively. Periodic checks encourage their memories and indicate the serious intent of the teachers. Require each student to keep an assignment notebook, and check them occasionally. Give practical tips on studying all through the year: how to use a text, how to read for different purposes, how to write for different purposes, how to be prompt with assignments, and how to pro-rate time.

Visits to local libraries, and learning to use different library systems strengthen students' abilities to find and use various sources of information. Explain common reference materials, and require their use in later assignments. Skills of outlining, making a bibliography, and writing footnotes should be included.

Assignments of many kinds give students a variety of experiences. Some can be made orally, with their notes checked later for accuracy. Some can be put on the overhead for copying. Long-term assignments might be dittoed. Be prepared to spend whatever time is required for explanation, so students will know the purpose of the assignment, exactly what they are to do, why, and by what completion date. Putting directions in writing settles many arguments, provides a reference, and helps students who have a short attention span. Posting a master copy will assist those who lose their own. In most assignments stress the necessity for following directions, but when creative interpretation is called for, encourage them to use their own initiative.

Opportunities will arise for students to assume responsibility within the classroom for various jobs, some of a recurring nature. Small groups may volunteer to collect material and arrange special bulletin boards on topics of interest. One member may check roll each morning. A group may assume complete charge of audio-visual material for the team. Each student can file his returned graded papers in folders in filing cases. At the end of each grading period, he can review his grades and make sure all assignments have been prepared. Such a check is also a good way for a student to mark his growth in learning over a period of time.

In addition to long-term problems of classroom performance, students face immediate questions posed by unknown people and new places. Many are lonely, and confused by the size of both building and student body. Locating rooms, sizing up teachers, struggling with lockers, and following a unique schedule, all at once, can be overwhelming.

To meet immediate student needs, the team of teachers may begin the year with assurances, maps of the school, and dittoed instructions, often repeated. They may be called upon to help students solve problems, answer questions, interpret directions, explain rules, open recalcitrant lockers, rescue and return lost articles. They will need to explain schedules and the purpose of regulations which intially appear meaningless, refer complaints about bus troubles, and generally perform those functions the students themselves can assume with confidence after a short time. Confidence, like experience, leads to independence.

The team operation enables teachers to aid students with two other concerns, achievement and friends. How to be a better student can be emphasized, and, repeatedly throughout the year, steps can be taken to encourage the students to increase their efficiency. One way to help them is to establish a team assignment notebook containing absentees' names, each day's activities recorded by subject, and homework assignments. (See Appendix, "Assignment Notebook Form.") Absentees, upon their return, should be instructed to check the notebook, copy the assignments, and check off their names. Individual help should be provided for students who need it at this point.

Meeting student needs concerning friends is harder because the teacher's role has to be invisible and her methods indirect. She will counsel and encourage the lonely ones, being an adult prop until they no longer need her. She may want to suggest activities in which students can meet friends: extracurricular activities, committees, sports, groups working on party decorations and refreshments. In class operation she can use the familiar techniques of groupings and seating arrangements, assigning jobs and errands to allow students to work together, trying to make students acceptable and desirable as friends to other students, and recognizing students for *any* kind of positive accomplishment. Homeroom activities will help.

Many students will take advantage of the increased opportunities for friendship provided by the larger number of students in the team. Another plus is the carryover of cooperative spirit from general team scholastic efforts into social interaction. Most students will become flexible as a result of frequent changes in size and composition of groupings, and team members will be able to work together in many combinations. Friendships form between team members along usual lines. In addition, most of the students will feel both an identification with their homeroom and a strong loyalty to the team operation. They may express this in diverse ways: assistance with any job at hand, springing to the defense of a missing teammate, active concern for each other's problems, and a surprisingly mature empathy for team members as they struggle with difficult tasks, such as presenting an oral report before the large group.

Activities for Various Group Sizes

Arrangements of student groups may be determined by student ability, by the activity involved, or by the size appropriate to a given objective. Chapter 2 suggests ways to utilize ability grouping to accomplish particular goals.

It is easy to relate activities to time and group sizes because so many guidelines exist. For example, it is logical to expose the total group together to those items required of all: tests and pretest reviews, common assignments, general instructions, and audio-visual presentations. Certain activities by their very nature limit group sizes. It is disastrous to learning to schedule into a lab or a skill-building exercise more students than the teacher can help individually.

Groups intermediate in size between a standard classroom number and a total team can engage in many of the same kinds of activities as those of a standard classroom. Working with this size group a teacher can introduce new material; give instructions; conduct discussions, debates, contests; and carry on the kind of class in which an assignment is introduced, carried out, and collected all in one class period. Surprisingly the larger size of the group will have little effect on these kinds of tasks and on teaching techniques.

Small groups are especially suited for exploring questions of policy, of choice, of opinion. Oblivious to other groups around it, each cluster of students can debate the question at hand, keep records, and hammer out a consensus with room for dissent before reporting its findings back to the team. Student autonomy gradually develops until the teacher becomes superfluous to the group purpose. Student enthusiasm for this type of activity is unquenchable.

One unique use for a small group is a group-counseling session. While other team teachers handle the majority of the students, one teacher and/or the counselor or another administrator may confer with a small number of students who have a common problem. An individual who is unable to discuss his problem alone with an adult may take courage from the support of his peers. Such an arena enables students to air complaints, to listen to each other, and to make suggestions for solving communication difficulties. (See Appendix, "Summary of Activities Suitable for Different-Sized Groups.")

Use of Time

The total amount of time scheduled for the team will vary with the individual situation, but will probably be the equivalent of one daily class period for each of the teachers involved. Ideally this amount of time will be in a consecutive uninterrupted block. But in order to make the most of the time available to the team, its teachers must force themselves to stop thinking of periods of standard class length.

Instead, think positively of the lessons you want to present, and the ideal length of time you need for each. All good teachers have suffered the frustration of having the bell interrupt a good lesson at a crucial point. The dissatisfaction of all the class members with such an interruption was vividly portrayed in the book, *Up the Down Staircase.* Standard class periods treat class activities like the victims of the Procrustean bed. Once you get over the shock of not having to tailor your lesson to an arbitrary time period, you can relax and enjoy your new-found freedom. You can use time to suit *your* needs.

All kinds of exciting things can happen. The removal of time restrictions creates an infectious enthusiasm within the entire team. How many times have you and your class been in the midst of an exciting discussion or debate, only to have to break it off and try to pick up the pieces the next day when the mood is lost? Or, on the other hand, how often have you launched into a lesson only to discover that this just wasn't the day to introduce grammar? But you had to plod resolutely through it to fill up the class period.

In a team teaching situation the delightfully flexible use of time and teacher cooperation obviate these horrors. You can continue your discussion beyond the team time allotted, or if desired, end a lesson that just isn't "jelling" and move on to other activities.

If you decide to shorten a session abruptly, there are a number of alternatives, whether or not other team teachers are free to help. A good teacher will always have tucked away in her file a collection of adaptable ideas. This is a good opportunity for their use. You can assign homework reading to be begun in class. Or you can find out why the lesson didn't jell. The teacher may learn something about the presentation, or she may find they all went to a basketball game the night before. Or you can listen to the students, who always claim that no one ever listens to them. The few minutes you can squeeze in for informal guidance may be far more valuable than any lesson you might have scheduled. You might even go so far as to ask students for suggestions for improving the team operation. This question should be reserved for those occasions when you have long periods of empty time to fill.

When one team teacher has a large- or intermediate-sized group and a lesson flops, some other team teacher will often be free to step in and help. She may need the amount of time left for going over a set of returned papers. She may want to use it to emphasize some small part of a previously taught lesson, which is still causing many students difficulty. One of the team teachers may need to use the time for housekeeping chores or for making an assignment. She might step in with an idea which was sparked by the first lesson, and lead a discussion down a worthwhile track. Finally, the team teachers in charge of the group may decide to give the children the time to use for study, or for free reading. If students have learned always to come to class prepared, they will have all their necessary tools, and can get a headstart on homework, or simply lose themselves in a book.

On some days, no amount of time is sufficient to accommodate all the student enthusiasm. Some films trigger this intense student interest. Questions asked of a guest speaker often require more time than you've planned. Sometimes special treatment of an ordinary theme will raise it to such a plateau of excitement that time simply evaporates. In one large-group session, considering the question, "Did young people have more chance to be courageous and independent in colonial times than they do now?", the authors experienced such protracted and intense student interaction that the class voluntarily continued the discussion even though their lunch hour had begun.

When particularly difficult material is being explored, you may feel that just a little more time would enable the class to reach the "Oh, *now* I see" stage. So, take that additional bit of time; team teaching permits it. Another unexpected need for additional time might occur when a student draws from first-hand experience to enrich a class study, thus extending the lesson beyond its anticipated length. The team situation allows for this, too. Most teams will include a budding authority on rocks, a baseball enthusiast, a boy who's handy with tools and machinery, a student who has lived in the foreign country under study. All teachers have had to cut short an eye-witness account of real student interest in their zest to cover a lesson. Team teaching permits these worthwhile contributions to enhance the learning.

Perhaps a word is in order about your first excursion into variable use of time. Teachers new to team teaching may feel hesitant to break the familiar pattern of meeting every group every day for the same amount of time. They may fear that if one day passes in which they miss seeing a class of students, those students will never catch up to the others.

Consider seeing fewer groups for longer periods of time some days, and not at all on others. See the rest of the classes on other days. Give thought to a large-group presentation one day with time for small-group follow-up or individual pursuit the following day. Meeting each class every day is not the magic formula. The concept of a story line in narrative poetry might be introduced in the large group one day. On the following day, time may be scheduled for individuals to read and write narrative poetry in standard-sized groups. This introduction to poetry is just as effective as the more traditional system. (See the Appendix for examples of individual teacher and student time usage schedules and forms for weekly schedule plans and weekly audio-visual requests.)

Given vision and courage, the number of possible grouping variations is limitless. Trial and error will quickly reveal which activities are suited to different group sizes and time periods. Seeing a child at work in different groups of different sizes and at varying tasks will present a far truer picture of him than could be gained under less varying circumstances. This broader view will enable the teacher to meet more fully the particular needs of the student, and this is one of the greatest of the many advantages of team teaching.

4   Relationships

When you fall into a man's conversation,
the first thing you should consider is,
whether he has a greater inclination to
hear you, or that you should hear him.

Sir Richard Steele

What about the possibility of your being involved in team teaching? What are the questions you might face regarding the type of people with whom you would be working? What is the team teacher's role, individually and as a team unit, with regard to the other staff members, administrators, and all special service personnel? How can the total school staff work together most effectively to reach the shared goal of helping students learn? These and other questions bombard the teacher facing the prospect of entering team teaching. Not all teachers feel they would be most effective working in a team. Some believe, and rightly so perhaps, that they work best alone. Over the years many of these have found comfortable procedures which may be difficult or even impossible to change. Since team teaching requires flexible and imaginative teachers, with facility for compromise, it may be difficult for some teachers to adapt to this kind of organizational pattern.

All of us face a challenging array of personal relationships in all realms of our lives. When limited to team teaching, there are certain unique "basics" that must evolve if the team is to function within the optimum range. A comfortable working climate and a cooperatively established set of ground rules is necessary. Individual and team responsibilities must be defined. Provision must be made for maintaining each member's individuality without sacrificing the unity of the group.

Within the Team

One of the areas of greatest concern to teachers preparing for team teaching is personal relationships within the team. As in any closely operating unit, these relationships are extremely important. The team must function as a unit without sacrificing the personality and techniques of the individual teachers involved. How, then, may this be accomplished? First, a comfortable working climate should be considered essential (see Fig. 11). Each group, of course, must establish its own working climate. For some, this means:

(1) Honest discussions together of doubts, fears, and concerns, as well as excitements and enthusiasms.

(2) Freedom to question, disapprove, or express delight concerning any of the team activities.

(3) Freedom to speak frankly about personal reactions to each other, without feeling threatened.

A trend, sometimes referred to as Sensitivity Training or T-Grouping, is gathering momentum nationally. Its techniques stress close personal relationships. It strives to enable individuals to relate to others openly and to understand their own

Figure 11. *Team teachers need a regularly scheduled team planning time. Usage of time and group sizes will absorb part of the time. Another part will be spent discussing ways to overlap and inter-relate particular learnings. An opportunity to preview filmstrips together will enable the group to use the aids more effectively. Most important of all is the chance to discuss the individual students and to plot ways to work together to meet their needs.*

motivations more clearly. Trained group leaders are generally required for these sessions. While the goals of this type of program are desirable, the individual team can attain these same goals through determined effort to establish an open climate.

Like a close family unit, you and your teammates must first care about each other as people. You must be willing to listen to each other and be interested enough to help. At first, such openness may be threatening and seem impossible to achieve. You may feel insecure or disinterested. But the resulting atmosphere is worth the effort since it will permit a more complete and more honest exchange within the framework of your team. And, in interpreting your teammates to other teachers you may improve total staff relations.

The fact that this climate has once been established does not guarantee that it will continue. Like freedom, you must work to maintain it. If you fail to keep the personal communication channels open your relationships may bog down in edginess, suspicion, and irritability toward each other. The comfortable working climate may disappear until it is restored through frank discussion.

It bears repeating that each set of team teachers must develop its own working climate. While some groups may prefer openness and total candor, others may choose a less direct relationship. The group's selection of the level of involvement may lie at any point along the continuum of frankness.

The degree to which an individual teacher feels comfortable and free with her team cohorts directly influences the level at which the total team of teachers can function. A teacher unsure of her subject matter, one with discipline problems, one accustomed to teaching "off the top of her head" may resent or may feel defensive at the thought of teaching in front of her peers. On the other hand the members of an effective, closely knit team may relish the opportunity to observe and learn from each other.

The cry through the ages has been that teachers, too often isolated from other teachers and their techniques, tend to become stagnant in their teaching. Almost no opportunity exists for the classroom teacher to observe other teachers at work. Within the team framework constant observation of other teachers as they work with the same students under the same basic conditions furnishes an arena for individual teacher growth far beyond one's wildest expectations. Rather than feeling threatened by being constantly evaluated by other team members, individuals enjoy being supported by the interest they have in each other.

While a presentation is occurring, other teachers will probably find themselves "pulling with" the teacher in charge. Because the goals of the lesson have been jointly planned, the assisting teachers are in an ideal position to further their attainment. A well-timed question or an enriching comment may offer support to the teacher presenting the lesson. In addition, daily emergencies that occur in an ordinary classroom cease to disrupt the entire class. Audio-visual equipment breakdowns, students with emotional upsets who need immediate help or ill students can be handled by the supporting teachers. One of the team teachers can simply step in to smooth the way, thus freeing the teacher in charge to continue with the lesson.

At first glance, the role of the team teacher seems irreconcilable since she must work both to establish an effective group and also to maintain her individuality. This dichotomy is not impossible to resolve and it *can* be done. By way of example, we have all known families where a climate permitting frankness and straightforwardness was established and enabled the group to think and feel as a unit. But at the same time, the role of each individual in that family and their unique abilities remained all important. This is indeed the type of relationships team teaching affords.

It is imperative that teachers involved in teams speak as *individuals* and not always as a team. This gives other staff members and administrators an opportunity to react to the *one* teacher, not the whole team. A totally cohesive "we-ness" discourages such interaction. Consensus of opinion and the sharing of some basic values by team teachers are fine; however, it is possible and desirable to maintain differences and independence. The spirit of respect possible within a group of teachers may make this easy to do, but team teachers and administrators should be critically aware of the constant pull of consensus versus independence.

Since team teaching requires more time, some team teachers may find that too many responsibilities, both in school and out, preclude adequate functioning as a team member. Each group must decide how to handle excessive individual responsibilities which might cripple the final product of their efforts. In spite of the pull of other staff activities, team teachers must place

first professional priority on team duties, or they will frustrate
and disturb the other members. A member who serves as
chairman of his academic department, is taking college courses,
and is writing curriculum for next year would be hard pressed
to be a valuable contributing member of a team. He would
rarely be present for team meetings or parent conferences. A
solution might be hammered out in the group, *if* the teachers
have established the open climate discussed previously. He
might be helped to see that his responsibilities to the group are
not being met and steps worked out for him to meet them.
Perhaps deleting some of his other jobs would remedy the
situation.

Conversely, excessive group demands may be unfair to certain individuals and this should be grappled with in the group
meetings. Each member should bear a fair share of the load,
within the limits of his or her own unique talents and abilities.

It would be pleasant if the team teachers could concentrate
solely on ideas, content, and children. Unfortunately, however,
chores must be performed to insure efficient operation. Dividing
the responsibilities for such duties among several teachers is
an economical use of time. One teacher can arrange for all
audio-visual equipment and materials (a suggested request
form for this purpose is included in the Appendix). If team
lesson plans and weekly schedules must be submitted to the
principal, one member can handle this duty. Be sure to keep
a copy of such materials for the team's reference. If a daily or
weekly bulletin board is to be part of your planning, designate
one member for this assignment. A cumulative calendar of
all-school and special team dates will be an invaluable contribution from one team member. Since all team teachers will
decide together on procedures, they will be aware of their
directions and there is no necessity for each to perform the
same routine duties.

When dividing these responsibilities, another consideration
is teacher interest. Not only can skills in a given discipline
be effectively utilized, but also, personal interests and abilities
come into focus and serve to relieve the others of these

assignments. Certain records and reports have to be kept and the team member who most enjoys this kind of activity may volunteer to handle this area. Many contacts with other teachers, counselors, and school personnel will be necessary and can be handled by one who likes doing this. The teacher whose interests include preparation of visual aids, transparencies, etc., can prepare such aids for everyone on the team. In working directly with students, one teacher may be more adept at presentations to large groups while another may have a real gift for working with very small groups.

In any classroom much time is spent on announcements, general explanations, and similar chores related to school activities. One teacher may be especially capable of functioning in this area. Many occasions exist for group guidance: pursuing ideas, exploring problems, expressing opinions. The teacher with a special knack for this kind of work can obtain effective results with students. Hopefully, the strengths, weaknesses, and interests of your group will dovetail.

As the year progresses, you will become a more closely operating team unit. New abilities will be discovered and utilized and you will be able to shift responsibilities. Watching the methods someone else uses to work with small groups may tempt you to try. Seeing effective use of transparencies may encourage you to create and use them in your teaching. This opportunity to share duties is a decided advantage of team teaching.

Some teams may desire to designate a leader or contact person. Such an arrangement enables other staff members to get in touch with the group more easily. A leader may be needed to keep the group functioning efficiently, to begin the meetings and to assign responsibilities. However, some teams may feel no need for a leader. The repartee and exchange between members may be so free that they progress without a formal leader. In some instances, no one may want to serve as leader. Members may prefer equality and autonomy. They may be unable to agree on a leader. This choice is part of the overall decision each group must make about its functioning.

Like any organization, team teachers work more smoothly together once a set of ground rules is agreed upon. Such rules can eliminate areas of possible friction between teammates. While each group of team teachers will need to make its own rules, some disagreements may be avoided by considering problems common to many teams.

One such concern is the need for each teacher to preserve her own classroom style, in spite of the temptation to adopt techniques and traits she sees working so well for her teammates. She may even need to resist peer pressure to change some inimical qualities, unless the group agrees ahead of time on the inviolate right of each team member to teach in his or her own way.

As a corollary, each teacher needs to feel free to innovate as she desires, without threatening the rest of the group by such variety. The teacher who does not want to try new things at this time must also feel secure in not doing so.

Punctuality and faithful attendance at team meetings is another possible bone of contention. Groups work better if time usage is agreed upon and reliably adhered to.

One of the strengths of any team, the diversity of talent possessed by its teachers, is also a source of potential discord. Each member will have her own understandings of the extent to which she wants to interrelate her own discipline or subject matter to those of the rest of the group. If the members can agree to respect each other for what they are and for the unique talents they possess, then the degree of cooperation that occurs will be voluntary cooperation between two or more teachers, at a propitious moment. No one will feel required to force a blending just because someone else is doing so. Freedom from pressure will encourage the irresolute and protect the neophyte.

In order to strengthen the whole team operation, a team's teachers can agree at the beginning of the year to help substitutes and teacher aides, whenever a regular staff member is absent. Location of supplies, identification of students who perform special jobs or possess exceptional handicaps, seating charts, team schedules, and the like are all examples of the type of aid which enables a substitute to pull her share of the team load.

With Other School Personnel

After team members establish the foundation for cooperation within the team, it is time to consider ways of improving relationships with all other school personnel.

In Chapter 1, the administrator's role was delineated as both complementary to the teacher's and strongly supportive. His crucial functions provided a climate of freedom to operate within, and included assistance with time, funds, and encouragement, as well as evaluation of teaching attempts.

He may do more. A principal who is experienced in team teaching, or a superintendent or curriculum director proficient in group instructional skills may supply a team with techniques and ideas of incalculable worth. Sometimes it is helpful just to be able to talk over an idea with a knowledgeable person; the pieces fall into place and order and cohesion develop. If you are really lucky, the meeting of minds will spark a flood of creativity.

Another priceless commodity a good principal affords his teachers is his support when they are under attack. As mentioned before in Chapter 1, change in the public schools sometimes causes repercussions in the community. When parents misunderstand, or are unaware of, a team's goals, team teachers may suffer sharp invective. While it is a parent's right to have a say in his child's education, his criticism may devastate a teacher who is conscientious. The aware principal acts as a buffer, listening to the concerned parent, yet protecting his teacher from unfair accusations made in the heat of a parent's anxiety. A staff which lacks this kind of administrative protection may choose to plod along well-worn paths rather than innovate and risk the disapproval of some parents.

The concept of team teaching with its many ramifications and forms may be difficult to understand. To achieve maximum cooperation between special school personnel and the team teachers, the team program must be explained to all. Specific ways for others to help should be indicated. Conscious efforts must be made to *work with* supportive personnel rather than just to *use* their services. The custodians, for example, will approach the daily furniture rearrangment more cheerfully if they understand the need for such things as small groups, large screens, and circular seating. When a teacher aide is asked to arrange student papers for more efficient return, she will be more understanding if the mass of the team is clear in her mind. And secretaries will place more emphasis on the clarity of announcements and time deadlines if they realize the complexity of working with a large block of students.

The contributions which a counselor can make to a team were discussed in earlier chapters. In relations with all guidance personnel, a teacher should keep in mind the variances in their basic approaches to children. While a large share of the teacher's time concerns a student's action in the group, the counselor relates on a one-to-one basis with a student. Observing students in assorted roles and groups contributes to the growth of both teacher and counselor as they work together for the betterment of the student.

Speech therapists, school nurses, visiting teachers and other specialists supplement the team teacher. For these services to be most beneficial, the scheduling should allow student departure at a propitious time.

If your team has scheduled a test, a film, or a one-time presentation which cannot be made up, inform the specialists well in advance. In this way, they can schedule appointments at some other time. But as a usual rule, be flexible. Cooperate in scheduling student meetings with these professionals. Remember, too, that great demands are made on a specialist. The specialist may serve several buildings, may have to use any vacant space available for work, and the schedule may include many more than the ideal number of student contacts.

One often overlooked way of helping special teachers understand the team program is to invite them to a class session. The speech therapist can offer specialized and interesting information to a science class studying sound or to an English class learning the importance of projection.

The school nurse should become familiar to the team. Aside from her usual contacts with them she, too, may consent to teach occasionally. Her knowledge of health and medicine can augment the content of a study of dietary problems during the Westward movement or her techniques for working with students can make a sex education study more authoritative. If a team teacher is cooperative, the interrelationships with special personnel can not only be pleasant but can also be productive.

Just as a team may enjoy pleasant relationships with school supportive personnel by knowing their schedules, so it is possible to obtain audio-visual materials efficiently by understanding proper procedures. Friction reducers should be employed. One possibility is a schedule on which all users of material sign up, and to which all users adhere. Any teacher who does not create some kind of system can wreck widespread havoc. Personnel in charge of audio-visual grow bitter at teacher complaints and staff disregard of their problems. Teachers need to be flexible enough to change their lesson plans when, despite the best efforts of the audio-visual department, a scheduled film does not arrive. If there are repeated unexplained delays, perhaps a three-way conference with the principal may produce a solution.

Use of a reading specialist can provide help desperately needed by students weak in reading skills. Because the ability to read well is so basic to school success, a team may need to schedule the students' visits to the reading specialist before it plans other team activities. Both team and specialist will profit from close adherence to the schedule jointly arranged. Both can contribute to serene relationships by advance notice if there must be a change in the plans.

Undoubtedly, the most versatile special-service person for the team is the librarian or the learning-center specialist. She can provide a wealth of assistance to team students and teachers, ranging from pulling books to making presentations.

As a portion of a team's orientation program for students, the librarian can introduce them to the learning center and clearly outline: its policies; the location of its books, magazines, and card catalogue; use of special reference books and equipment such as individual filmstrip projectors, microfilm viewers, and record players. When this orientation is well done with large visual aids and activities for the students to perform, interest in the learning center is high.

With the increased stress on independent study, the librarian's role as a resource person or an assistant-to-the-search for students is vital. She may not only make available all books and information in the school's learning center but she may garner materials from sources such as the community or state libraries. Each student on independent study should carry a prospectus and proposal of his outline of study to assist the learning center personnel in offering meaningful assistance.

Other aids to students might include distribution of reading lists and the sale of paperback books, of particular interest to young people. The Junior Great Books Course,* with its emphasis on interrelating major ideas, may supplement the team's activities. The learning-center specialist is the ideal person to conduct such a group.

Another valuable service is the direct assistance to teachers which can come into play at any point of the planning schedule. The librarian may meet with the team teachers to discuss future lessons. She may supply some broad suggestions and also give concrete advice as to the materials available in the learning center about a particular topic. She may pull all books and magazines related to this topic and display them on a book cart. This arrangement not only makes it easy to transport the materials to necessary locations, but it also serves as a focal point of interest to students. The librarian may compose a list of materials available for a unit. This list may include all audio-visual supplements as well as printed matter. Such services can endear the librarian to the teaching staff.

---

*Great Books Foundation, 307 North Michigan Avenue, Chicago, Illinois 60601.

Time permitting, the librarian can keep teachers informed of the newest publications in their field and can notify them of receipt of such materials.

If adequate resources are *not* available to help a teacher make a salient point to a class, the librarian is the person best suited to assist with ordering. Certainly, she has at her fingertips such sources as *Books in Print* to aid in judicious decisions concerning purchases. Her knowledge of available monies (government or other) makes possible quick and efficient securing of materials.

In sum, team teaching relationships resemble other close associations. Tact and patience are required. A liberal sprinkling of compromise will ease the inevitable conflicts which arise. Levity lightens the load. Keep in mind that in a smoothly operating team your concerns and those of your teammates are identical.

5

Check-Up
Time

O wad some power the giftie gie us
To see oursels as others see us!
It wad frae monie a blunder free us,
An' foolish notion.

Robert Burns

Periodic evaluations improve any program, but are especially vital when you try something different. Both formal and impromptu assessments are valuable guides to a team's health and progress. Team teachers will want to check both their own and their students' growth. In addition, a great deal can be learned by listening to others: students, administrators, parents, and fellow teachers. The actions and comments of all these people give us the mirror Robert Burns so poetically longed for. Sometimes the image is a shocker, but it is always real.

65

By Staff

Teachers in every kind of classroom situation need to assess pupil progress, and team teachers have this need too. Many books cover such testing and evaluation. But what of the unique goals of a team, particularly an interdisciplinary one? It's easy to find out whether a child can divide by a two-digit number, but how do you check his progress toward self-confidence in speaking to a large group? What instrument is useful in measuring pupil ability in interrelating disciplines, following directions, transferring those skills learned in one area into a different field, contributing to the team, assuming ever increasing responsibility for himself and his behavior in a variety of group situations? Teachers on a team must develop their own evaluating materials to avoid the pitfall of wishful thinking. However laudable the goals, parents and administrators want and deserve more than subjective measurements.

Luckily, there are ways, and they need not be formal. As soon as administrators and parents are sure you have specific goals in mind, they'll go along. But they want to know how you know when you've reached them.

Teaching students to interpret oral and written instructions, for example, is a worthwhile objective and can be measured. Most teachers have run across the set of written directions that begins "Don't do anything until you read all the directions on this page" and proceeds to list things to do. The last direction negates the others and tricks the unwary, once. Most students are willing to play this game with a teacher, and many do it very well, because they see it as a game, not as "something that counts for a grade." But there is no carryover into everyday classroom activities. The obvious answer is to make following directions pay off. In a team as in square dancing, the one who goes the wrong way confuses the others. The habitual daydreamer, the gossiper, and the disorganized student will have difficulty learning this skill. These types challenge other students who want the team to operate effectively, to take forthright action. Such group pressure is a strong ally for the teacher, encouraging all to listen to instructions that all are to follow *jointly*.

Subtler means are necessary to cope with student disregard for such requirements as deadlines, appropriate methods in problem solving, stipulated length, proper form for bibliography, specified number and variety of sources for a paper, method of recording data, etc. The problem is to make such adult values important to the student, if only because he lives in a society which prints its last name first, in triplicate. One of the many advantages of team teaching is that once a team's teachers agree upon a goal, there are several minds at work, and the team's students hear the same thing from each staff member. It is a real joy to dispense forever with the ploy, "But you're the *only* teacher who makes me. . ."

This concerted approach, in every assignment and using a variety of methods, is quite effective in teaching the importance of interpreting instructions. Slowly but surely, students learn that it saves time to listen or read carefully, they don't have to redo assignments, grades improve, and lessons take less time. How can you tell when the message is received? There are many ways. Most of the papers on any given assignment come in on time and as specified. The students comment to each other, "Didn't you hear her? She said you could use any source *but* an encyclopedia. Now you'll have to do it over!" Students catch the teacher in inconsistencies (hard to take but indicating that they are listening). Students take time when an assignment is first made to ask about instructions they're not sure of and request additional guidelines if the teacher has omitted them. Students approach the teacher with pride, holding out a paper due that day, and pointing out all the ways they have followed directions. Setting these seemingly stringent requirements at the outset pays vast dividends to the students. They soon see that establishing a system for studying enables them to move quickly on to the equally important and far more interesting creative endeavors. The idea is not to make robots of youngsters, but rather to increase their effectiveness as individuals, especially in the school climate.

Being alert to student reactions supplies many valuable insights. Feedback thrives in a class atmosphere in which students are free to question, disagree, innovate, and meet staff on a person-to-person basis. If a questing student gets verbally flattened, the quest, and with it his progress toward self-responsibility in the classroom, will often end. The climate must be as comfortable for the child as for the adult, and that automatically means occasional discomfort for each, and the freedom of both to err without meeting sarcasm or horrified reproach.

Progress toward goals other than following directions can be measured in equally objective ways, but the measuring instruments have to be made as you go along. Each goal has to be broken down into specific behaviors, which can be observed, measured, and sometimes even quantified for statistically minded parents. For a goal such as the ability to interrelate disciplines, you look for such evidence as the following: (1) the end of questions such as, "What are we doing now, social studies or English?"; (2) the cessation of gripes about the unfairness of grading down for spelling errors on a science paper; and (3) student answers to all kinds of student questions indicating their application of skills and facts learned from one teacher to a discipline taught by another. For example, they see that proper footnote form for a social studies report is identical with that on last week's English paper. Or someone points out that, if you can't remember the exact date of a scientist's discovery, you can figure out roughly when it had to be from what you learned in history of the scientist's contemporaries. Watching a Cartesian diver in a science demonstration, students ponder the versatility of the Frenchman who also dreamed up ways to record math data for graphing, learned in a previous math lesson.

Similarly you evaluate transfer of skills between disciplines by noting certain clues. Changes in communication skills in classes other than English become evident. Increasing facility of students with the math part of science and ease in spotting science problems which can be quantified appear. Problem-solving approaches learned in science begin to be applied to nonscience problems. Students use the social studies multisource approach in developing opinions and value judgments in all areas of school life.

Increasing pupil responsibility for himself and others is not a goal unique to team teaching; however in a team there are different ways for a student to demonstrate such growth. The larger number of students involved makes classroom mechanics more time-consuming. But it also provides more opportunities for students to step in and help. Distributing and collecting books, pamphlets, and papers, keeping records of various kinds, setting up and dismantling audio-visual equipment, moving furniture can all be facilitated and improved upon by student assistance. One reliable measure of student responsibility is the spontaneous help supplied by pupils who have learned to see a job and get up and do it, without waiting to be asked. Another criterion is the increasing assumption by the children of both the conduct of the class and the direction their learnings are to take. Again, as responsibility increases, the need for teacher disciplinary action decreases. The class approaches the desired goal, a joint pursuit of learning.

So much for evaluation of students. How about staff measurement of its own accomplishments? In one sense, student growth represents staff accomplishment. But in another sense, each staff member will want to work on her own particular strengths and weaknesses as a teacher, and the team can help her in the dual jobs of assessment and improvement. Team teaching offers a staff the chance to teach in many different ways. As teachers experiment and innovate, both their latent talents and weaknesses become evident.

Working in the classroom with constant support and assistance from other team teachers, a staff member can feel courageous enough to try new things, or even to fail. Evaluating daily, weekly, monthly in sessions with these same supporters, a teacher can more readily face those faults which prevent the accomplishments she longs for. From these same cohorts she can get suggestions for ways to surmount the weaknesses. She will be helping each of the others with the same types of evaluation, so she needn't feel singled out, or diminished in her own eyes or theirs. While it is never easy or comfortable to be judged, it is possible to take criticism from colleagues wholeheartedly engaged with you in a common quest, particularly when these same allies do everything possible in the classroom to facilitate your teaching. The combination is an ideal one both for releasing innovative energy, and for promoting teacher growth. This camaraderie is especially valuable for the teacher who is experienced yet insecure in her professional life. The benefits to the first-year teacher, the student teacher, and the substitute are immeasurable.

Because some teachers fear and misunderstand this close peer association, they may try to avoid it. In so doing, they may unwittingly pass up an unexcelled opportunity for self-evaluation and growth. It is an exciting experience to watch a cohort teaching team students with fresh techniques. All teachers, even good ones, can improve their teaching styles by learning new "tricks of the trade" from others. Also, watching an expert at her craft sensitizes the alert staff member to new student interactions in the classroom. Finally, watching another teacher trigger a reaction in a student who has been lethargic in other groups, a teacher learns what to do to strike more responsive chords in children. Teachers have all been alone in their classrooms so long, they hesitate to share the load. When they cautiously try the change, they find not fear but relief, excitement, joy, and the satisfaction of growing again, both as persons and as teachers. Watching others teach broadens the criteria by which a teacher measures her own professional skills. But it does more; simultaneously it offers assistance in overcoming the weaknesses the watcher finds in her teaching.

A teacher should steal time to get off by herself and think through each day's activities. She should consider such points as: "What made this lesson really click?" "Was it the red I was wearing?" "What were the magic ingredients that finally hooked that sleepy little boy in the third row?" "Were those visual aids really worth the time and effort I spent on them?" "What *am* I

going to do about the two talkers?" "Why was it so difficult for
the class to understand the relationships in the graph I drew?"
"Shall I call Johnny's mother to see when he had his last hearing test?" "How can I best utilize the exciting sidetracks we
took yesterday?" And finally, "Did I really enjoy this day?"

Simply the fact that she has considered these points and
others like them is of value, and the analysis will offer her new
directions for self-improvement.

By Students

Student evaluations of the team tend to become more thorough and constructive as the children mature. If their honesty
and candor are encouraged, students as a group are capable of
fresh insights and a directness of approach that are most valuable to adults willing to listen. In addition to establishing the
receptive climate already mentioned, a team of teachers which
really wants student reaction can provide both formal and
informal opportunities.

Many structured instruments such as questionnaires and
scales exist for student use. Multiple-choice ratings offer a
range of comment, and encourage those allergic to pencil work
to take part. Open-ended sentences increase the variety of
responses possible in an evaluation. Sentences beginning, "I
think the team . . . " and "I wish the team would . . . " and
"Sometimes could we . . . " can be creatively finished in a surprising number of ways, perhaps even humorously. A short-
coming is that a pupil must dream up his own answers, and
may leave sentences unfinished if nothing comes to mind in a
hurry. (See Appendix for sample evaluation forms.)

Least structured of all written exercises is the blank-page
technique, coupled with a request for a listing of any comments
the student cares to make. Such an evaluation requires more
staff time than the others to tabulate and digest (an ideal job
for a teacher aide) because of the wide range of comments it
elicits. It also produces a sizable number of blank pieces of

paper, from students too comfortable to respond, or too lazy to complain.

Finally, there is the suggestion box, haven for the timid, the vitriolic, and the clever. These remarks, like all the others that are written, may be anonymous. (Signed comments of the poisoned-pen variety tell you your students trust you, whatever faults they may find.) In order that each student may be sure his suggestion has been read, the contents of the box, with appropriate answers, can be posted weekly on a team bulletin board. Answers to their questions enable the students to accept situations, because they know why they exist, and that needed changes will be made if possible.

In addition to student evaluation of team organization and program, their evaluation of teachers can offer an important contribution, often overlooked. While it is true that a child's opinion is more easily colored by his personal feelings, still the opinions of a group of children over a period of time are as valuable as those of adults. Children because of their immaturity may appreciate different qualities in team teachers than those which adults consider important. But students as young as ten are able to differentiate between the teacher they like because anything goes in her class, and the teacher whom they respect and learn from because her class is comfortable and fun yet productive. And pupils are remarkably clear-eyed in spotting adult sham, hypocrisy, unfairness, and dislike of children which masquerades as concern. Most children of twelve and thirteen are capable of a fair evaluation of an adult's qualities as a teacher, even when they dislike the adult as a person. Students contribute a unique point of view to teacher evaluation; there really is no one else who can tell us how things look to children. Whatever they say has some informative value for an adult working with them.

By Administrators

How is an administrator to appraise team progress? There are all the traditional ways, of course: classroom visitation, the student reports to counselors, report cards, and feedback from parents and teachers. He can check on use (or abuse) of audio-visual materials, and individual lesson plans. Conferences with student teachers, teacher aides, substitutes, and any secretaries whose services are available to the teachers and/or the students provide a certain amount of information to principals. Some sensitive and alert principals seem to know the general state of their schools through a sixth sense.

What additional evaluation sources does the team setup provide? An administrator can attend the planning meetings of a team's teachers, to learn about their projects and staff relationships. He can require the weekly submission of team lesson plans, for an overall view of a team's purposes. He can set aside time at staff meetings for teams to share problems and solutions, to air complaints, and to report on signal successes and failures. He can encourage innovation and experimentation. The results will not only be richly rewarding for all involved, but will also indicate the varying strengths and ingenuity of the teams. A good administrator constantly makes use of all these techniques, as he directs the operation of his school.

By Parents

Parent reactions seldom need to be solicited. They are as valuable and necessary a part of a team endeavor as of any other form of teaching. Parents evaluate almost entirely on one basis: "How does this affect my child?" If the community has been fully informed about team teaching before it is inaugurated (Chapters 1 and 6 discuss this at greater length), then parent concerns will be lessened, and they will have a sounder basis for assessment. If parents do not understand what is being done and why, they often view it as an experiment with their child's welfare, and they are apt to blame any and all difficulties their child may have in school upon the team organization. Ridiculous as this may sound, it is often true. It is wise to be prepared for this kind of criticism as parent misconceptions tend to be underestimated. An experienced teacher will probably be familiar with parent rationalization. To a first-year teacher, however, it is overwhelming to have the intelligent mother of a "problem child" look her right in the eye and insist that her son has, until this year, been a model of decorum, and that therefore, all his current misbehavior and lack of achievement must be due to the team operation.

In order to aid parents in making meaningful evaluations of team teaching, invite them to visit a large-group activity. Those who are convinced that team teaching means chaos; those who are concerned that their "sensitive" child will get lost in the large group; those who are certain that individual help will not be available; and in general those who tend to prejudge the team operation can profit by a first-hand view.

A final response to expect from parents is the demand to know what's so good about team teaching? "The old-fashioned way was good enough for me. Why isn't it good enough for my kids?" One answer is that team teaching is another way of trying to meet children's individual needs. There is no evidence that students do better academically as a result of team teaching, but neither is there evidence to show that they do worse. Previous experiences with control groups have shown that students involved in team teaching showed a higher level of: ability to transfer learnings; independence in study, in use of time, and in responsibility for their own behavior; self-control and self-reliance; initiative; awareness of their part in a bigger picture; organizational skills and sensitivity to the needs of others.

Conversely, when these same team students were compared with control groups, they were *less*: resistant to change; concerned with isolated facts; rigid about new ideas; shy about speaking before a group; reluctant to question and/or express opinions; patient with carelessness by students or teachers and restricted in student-teacher relationships.*

---

*Glenda Hanslovsky, Sue Moyer, and Helen Wagner, *Report of the Team Teaching Pilot Program* (Unpublished) (East Lansing Public Schools, 1967), pp. 39-40.

By Other Teachers

Estimates of other teachers concerning a team's functioning aid a team in measuring its effectiveness. If an entire school is team teaching, then teams will want to compare notes, and trade ideas, problems, and successes. Comparisons between teachers of different teams will be of a fairly casual nature, since each team will be primarily concerned with its own affairs.

On the other hand, if only some of the school's teachers and students are on teams, then team pursuits will be fairly closely observed by other staff members. Staff comments will serve as a barometer of opinion about the team.

Common reactions to expect under these circumstances are: interest from those teachers who are eager to try team teaching, criticism from those who fear innovation, misunderstanding from those who don't know what the team is trying to accomplish, and resentment from all who feel they're going to be forced to team teach whether they want to or not. Better communication at all levels is the best way to dispell illusions and to improve staff relationships.

Counselors are in a special position to provide worthwhile information to team teachers about students. Pertinent data about health, emotional problems, and parent attitudes is available to them. Without betraying any student confidences, counselors can pass along specific concerns, individual and/or widespread problems among the team students, conflicts with the rest of the school caused by some team function or method, etc. Counselors should attend team teacher planning sessions in order to understand team functioning better. They can interpret to the team teachers the effect on students of a particular team rule or practice, and in turn can help a student understand the reasons behind that procedure. Such cooperation can lead to worthwhile adjustments for both students and staff on a team. (See Chapter 4 for a more detailed treatment of relationships between team teachers and other adults concerned with education.)

The team students, parents, administrators and other staff within the school supply the four principal sources of outside opinion upon which team teachers can rely for evaluation. Occasionally an interested citizen or community group will add other information. Most of it is useful; all of it is informative. A team need never wonder about its image; it will be deluged by feedback from all sides. Truly professional team teachers will welcome evaluation and will profit from it.

6 Getting the Message Across

"The time has come," the Walrus
said, "to talk of many things."

Lewis Carroll

In all areas of endeavor today people agree that better communication is vital. The need to be clearly understood and cor-
rectly interpreted challenges not only the leaders of our nation,
the workers in industry, the members of a family, but especially
people involved in the education of our youth.

Communication is particularly important when innovation in
education is being considered. Team teaching may be partially
or entirely a new concept in many communities. Because of its
fluid nature, constant reinterpretation of the program is necessary. It is human nature to question, and often to object to
anything new. Once the philosophy and goals of a new organizational pattern are understood, greater acceptance and cooperation can be expected.

77

But you can never reach everyone, no matter how many meetings there are, or how much information is circulated. The use of frequent dittoed communications between teacher and parent concerning team plans and methods, shortens the time-consuming job of individual conferences with those parents who demand special attention, or who can't get all the information they want from their children. As soon as team teaching has been decided upon, steps should be taken to communicate with parents, students, and the community in general.

Parents

Of all the forms of communication needed, that involving the school and parents is most vital to the successful team operation. Parents both want and deserve to know about educational innovations affecting their children. They must be adequately informed both verbally and in writing.

One effective procedure is to issue a spring invitation to attend a meeting where the plan and procedures for the following year will be outlined. This meeting should present information and answer questions for parents of students who will enter the program the next fall. If such a meeting is scheduled for the evening, more fathers will be able to attend. Perhaps the principal, a counselor, and classroom teachers might present prepared information, but the bulk of the time should be free for questions from the floor. Although school personnel can probably anticipate the concerns of most parents, a question-and-answer session will insure that parents will receive some answers to their specific questions. They will also feel more immediate involvement in the project.

As soon as feasible after school begins in the fall, parents should be invited to an Open House. At this time the team teachers should present general information about regulations, methods of operation, the organizational pattern, activities, goals, grading systems, and specific suggestions for effective cooperation between school and home. Failure to explain these points early in the year may cause parents to blame the team operation for ordinary problems of adjustment to high school, the middle school, or the particular level of instruction. Ample time should be provided to assure parents of the teacher's interest in their child and to allay the fear that their child will lose some of his identity as he functions in a team.

During such a meeting pertinent and valuable information about the students can be secured. Their health conditions, special talents and interests, date of entry into the school system, and activities outside the school day can easily be written by parents on 3 x 5 cards. Keeping in mind that the more the teacher knows about the student in his class, the better he can aid his development, the value of this kind of information is clear. At this time, additional facts can also be procured concerning contributions the parents can make, such as their sharing of slides, collections, or knowledge; their assistance as chaperones for field trips, homeroom activities or social affairs; and their availability as tutors, classroom aides, or volunteers. (See Appendix for sample "Open House Form.")

As the year progresses, channels of communication must remain open and active. Regardless of the school's system of grading and reporting to parents, periodic progress reports can be used to advantage. A standard form supplied by the school will save the teacher much time. Such reports should be sent to the home to indicate exceptional progress in certain areas. Perhaps a more valuable service is the use of such reports to inform parents that their student is encountering difficulties at school. Specific observations contributing to this situation should be indicated. These might include failure to prepare daily assignments, poor performance on tests, reading problems, inability to function in a class, or indications of emotional upsets.

In the upper grades communication between parent and child is often a problem. Although students at these levels should be encouraged and helped to find solutions to their own problems, the parent should be made aware that such problems exist. (See Appendix for sample "Progress Report Form.")

Another method of communication with parents is the parent-teacher conference. Some schools schedule times during the first semester for such conferences with all parents. Other

systems use a more informal arrangement which permits either
the parents or the teacher to arrange a conference as the need
or the desire arises. The student's strengths, the areas needing
improvement, and his general adjustment to school and the
team may furnish the basis for such meetings. Parents may
choose to meet with all team teachers together or they may
prefer to see only a part of the group. Care should be taken to
insure that the parents feel comfortable in the situation rather
than overwhelmed by facing several teachers at once.

As soon as the schedule for parent-school contacts for the
year is established, parents should be informed of these dates.
Additional reminders prior to special events will bring about
better attendance and thus, the chance for clearer communication and greater cooperation.

It is a good idea to keep written and dated records of all
phone and personal conferences held with parents during the
year. Also it is helpful to a teacher to require that all notes sent
home regarding a pupil's progress be signed and returned to
her, as a record that they were received by the home. Both of
these suggestions pertain whether a teacher is on a team or not,
but they are particularly important whenever team teaching
is new to an area.

The field trip can also serve as an effective communication
link between home and school. To insure positive results certain procedures should be followed. First, obtain written permission for students to participate in field trips. This may relieve the teacher of liability in the event of accidents during
such trips. A standard form can be sent to all homes as part
of the registration procedure and will serve as permission for
the entire year. (See Appendix for sample field trip permission
form.) A few days before any field trip, however, a written
reminder concerning the destination, the date, and the means
of transportation should be sent to the home via the student.

Second, give parents an opportunity to assist with field trips.
Using the information obtained on the 3 x 5 cards at the Open
House and asking students to volunteer their parents will provide additional adults for supervision. A ratio of one adult to
each eight to ten students is desirable. The duties and responsi-

bilities of these supervisors should be clearly defined, and the responsibilities of students to the supervisors should also be stressed. Such opportunities for parent participation will afford a meaningful contact for parents and will also aid the teacher by permitting her to concentrate on instructional activities.

Students

Just as important as the preparation of parents for team teaching is the preparation of students. Before a student is to participate in a team, perhaps in the spring, he should have an opportunity to visit the school and talk with teachers and students about the team operation. A chance to see a team in action is desirable. Entire classes may be invited to join a team for a morning. Or the "buddy" system of visitation may be used. This enables students from the team to serve as buddies for visitors and thus to impart a personal touch which benefits both the host and the guest.

In order to help the new student feel at ease in the larger or different school, early notification of team assignment should be given. During the summer notices concerning team rooms, locker numbers, and team teachers can be mailed to the student. Through this method, opening day procedures are greatly simplified.

Another important form of communication with team students is an early introduction to the counselor or the homeroom teacher. Get-acquainted sessions with each individual should be scheduled as early in the school year as possible. This opens a door for the student and establishes some feeling of the personal interest of the school. The student will be more likely to initiate future contacts with counseling personnel if these initial conferences are held.

The Community

Since the majority of the community will be interested in educational directions in their area, inform the general public well in advance of the implementation of new programs. P.T.A. or any parent-school meetings will miss a large segment of the community, so all news media should be called upon. Newspaper articles with accompanying pictures, and radio or television interviews concerning team teaching will stimulate and inform the public.

Most service organizations in the community welcome speakers on topics of general educational interest. Study clubs, Kiwanis, Lions, Rotary, the Chamber of Commerce, and many other civic groups want to be informed about educational trends in their community. Church and community associations interested in youth development want to hear about educational practices and patterns for young people.

It is likely that teachers and administrators from neighboring schools will ask for someone to speak to their staffs about team teaching, and they most certainly will ask for visitation privileges once the project is under way. And don't be surprised if you are cornered at the grocery store, a bridge party, or neighborhood coffees to talk about team teaching. Now you see the importance of the reference in Chapter 1: "You must *really want* to be involved in team teaching."

Summary

Certain procedures are advisable when innovation is to occur in schools. Early and frequent communication between the school and the parents, the school and the student, and the school and the community will reassure those concerned that the team teaching approach offers exciting and worthwhile educational experiences and growth to students.

7

Why Team Teaching?

All you need in life is ignorance
and confidence, and then Success
is sure.

S. L. Clemens

Now that this discussion has explored what term teaching is, how to prepare for it, how to engage in it, and how to evaluate it, it is time to ask "but *why* team teaching?" Why is this organizational innovation desirable?

First, let it be clearly understood that team teaching is only one of many possible innovations and answers, not *the* answer to all problems plaguing teachers, students, and administrators. It does, however, have truly awesome advantages for all three of these groups.

For Teachers

One group, the teachers, may honestly wonder whether the extra time and effort required by team teaching will balance the advantages. A brief summing-up of all pertinent data may help them reach a decision:

1. Planning for actual instruction is increased and improvement of instruction results.

2. The number of times a presentation must be made decreases. Utilization of the total group can be made to show a movie or give a presentation once to all the team students. In essence, three or four separate classes can be exposed to material at the same time.

3. Allowance is made for better utilization of "specialists," consultants, and general resource persons.

4. Curriculum must be re-evaluated constantly, in light of each new goal.

5. Opportunities for flexibility are insured.

6. Expanded insights into the viewpoints and beliefs of others usually result.

7. The team framework provides an exciting way to teach, to innovate and to experiment with different methods, class sizes, groupings, and time usage.

8. Teacher strengths are utilized as each teaches his specialty.

9. Teachers can share ideas and polish materials before they are presented to students.

10. Provision can be made for time to talk shop: about children and their problems and what you can do about them; about exciting ways of presenting new information; about stimulating types of activities and assignments that are tantalizing to students.

11. Teachers gain many new techniques, approaches, etc., from watching other team teachers work with the same

students, under the same basic conditions.

12. Teachers are forced to re-evaluate *what* they are teaching and *why* they are teaching it.
13. Shared planning helps when burdens and pressures seem unreal.
14. Support is present for the neophyte and these new teachers can more quickly become a part of the school.
15. The invaluable assistance of respected co-workers in becoming a better teacher insures growth.
16. Talents develop that teachers never dreamed they had.

Although the advantages far outweigh the disadvantages for teachers, you may meet some of the following drawbacks:

1. Incompatible teammates.
2. Increased demands on your time and efforts.
3. Discouragement over failure to achieve all goals at the outset (it takes time; move slowly and don't expect perfection with your first efforts).
4. Exhaustion caused by the stimulation of constant interaction with peers.
5. Lack of parental cooperation in innovative undertakings.
6. Minimal understanding from the principal of his role in making team teaching work.

For Students

The life of the student today is very complex. He is surrounded by mushrooming knowledge, by rapid technical advances and by cultural changes. Some functions of the school are to help the student prepare for life in this changing world; to teach him the skills which he can apply; to assist him in learning to relate ideas, to transfer knowledge, in short, *to think.*

When considering the effects of team teaching on the student one should ask: In what skills can students grow? What kind of child functions most effectively in the team arrangement? To what extent can students increase their general awareness? How do the experiences of children in a team differ from those of children in other arrangements? Can behavioral changes be measured objectively? Academically, do students perform better, worse, or approximately the same? Most of these questions have been answered in the preceding chapters; however, let us summarize:

1. They are allowed to work at their own rate of speed and to do more independent study.

2. There is more unstructured time in which students may seek individual help from teachers and other special service personnel.

3. The interdependence of and the correlations between subject areas and disciplines are clarified for students.

4. Students are helped to gain a more independent attitude, and their activities indicate they can assume more responsibility than they are usually allowed.

5. Practice in speaking before various group sizes, large, medium, and small, helps students develop poise.

6. Students improve their discussion skills. Ideas are bounced around more freely, yet with more correlation than previously occurred between subjects. With stress on discussions in varying group sizes, students in the team setting exchange ideas with many more students than they could in traditional classrooms.

7. As teachers reinforce learnings in different disciplines by use of varied assignments, students grow in all basic skill areas.

8. Students become more adept in the skills of evaluation, both of their own work and that of others. With so many opportunities for comparison of techniques, they can judge teachers' performances more effectively.

Figure 12. *Does team teaching generate enthusiasm? Does the individual have a chance to participate? The picture speaks for itself.*

9. There is one set of common expectations by which to function in each team class, instead of different sets for each class.

10. Staff attention to student homework and test schedules guarantees that these are spaced rather than bunched.

11. Greater variety in the school day is possible.

Students will find few drawbacks in a team since it is an arrangement devised to facilitate their learning (see Fig. 12). One of the uncomfortable areas might be the feeling of increased competition with a larger group. Being part of a stimulating academic group for a part of the day may tire some students excessively. In the beginning, the extremely flexible schedule confuses the traditionally oriented student.

For Administrators

Since no team teaching venture can succeed without the support of the principal, the advantages to the administrator should be examined. While his duties remain much the same as those of a principal in a traditional school, they will be eased by inherent characteristics of the team pattern. The following points are among the advantages:

1. Scheduling of classes is easier since students and teachers are merely assigned to teams rather than to individual classes.

2. Curriculum will be assessed by the staff according to new, broad sights gained in their interactions.

3. Flexibility of time, room use, students, and teachers can be a by-product.

4. Teachers who are weak and those who are strong can be assigned to one team to balance each other. Such a system protects students from large inequities in instruction. This arrangement makes help available at all times for teachers who need it.

5. New teachers can be more quickly assimilated into a school program with less administrative time spent in the orientation process.

6. Meetings with team teachers can be planned easily, during their regularly scheduled team planning period.

7. Communications to the whole team are possible through one teacher.

8. Most of all, team teaching offers a golden opportunity for his staff to become better teachers while they teach, a kind of ready-made in-service program of benefit to the entire school.

Unfortunately, there are a few disadvantages for principals. The team organization will require more personal contact with both his faculty and the community. He will need to spend more time helping teachers make personal adjustments to the intimacy of the team arrangement. Because scheduling tends to segment his staff he must expend more effort creating a cohesive group to attack common problems. His skill as a leader will aid him as he visits teams in session, consults with teachers, and experiments with flexible scheduling. Questing parents will require more of his time as they seek explanations and reassurances about school innovation.

Summary

We must repeat that there is no formula which assures a successful team operation. Certain ingredients are essential, however.

1. Teachers and administrators must *really want* to be involved in team teaching.

2. Teachers must develop the patience and the talent to blend their attitudes and abilities, and to accept each other's values while retaining their individuality.

3. The staff must have the willingness to devote extra time to planning, daily revamping, and to allowing each member to utilize his own techniques for thinking through decisions concerning group efforts.

Team teaching is not a static situation. It is dependent on the dedication of the administrator and the make-up of each team in each school system. Success of team teaching is limited only by the vision, the initiative, and the ability of the individual teachers within the team.

In a precise answer to the question posed by the title, "Why Team Teaching?", three benefits have special pertinence to today's educators. First, the team organizational pattern enables teachers to be more cognizant of each individual student's needs, since the impressions of several teachers contribute to the composite picture of each child. Second, our freedom to innovate in both curriculum and time usage permits the teachers to individualize instruction to a greater extent and to encourage independent study for those students able to profit by it. Finally, it allows the administrator to implement a variety of educational programs of value to teacher and student.

Team teaching is an exciting and challenging experience. It is good for the students; it has many benefits for teachers and administrators as well. Removal of the boundaries of disciplines encourages the student to interrelate one subject with others. Traditional school experiences, compartmentalized into English, mathematics, social studies, and science are unreal when compared with the kaleidoscopic patterns of life itself. The approach to learning offered by team teaching enables the student more readily to make the transfer from "school learnings" to "life applications." This transfer is a major goal of educators, both teachers and administrators. Team teaching offers one avenue for pursuit of this goal.

With this book as a guide and with your own creativity and desire to innovate, you can now proceed. Soon, you will be able to supply your own answer to the question, "Why team teaching?".

BIBLIOGRAPHY

BOOKS

Blair, Medill, and Richard G. Woodward, *Team Teaching in Action,* Boston: Houghton Mifflin Company, 1964.

Beggs, David W., III, ed., *Team Teaching — Bold New Venture,* Indianapolis: Unified College Press, Inc., 1964.

Eichhorn, Donald H., *The Middle School,* New York: The Center for Applied Research in Education, Inc., 1966.

Fenton, Edwin, *Teaching the New Social Studies in Secondary Schools: An Inductive Approach,* New York: Holt, Rinehart and Winston, Inc., 1966.

Grooms, M. Ann, *Perspectives on the Middle School,* Columbus, Ohio: Charles E. Merrill Books, Inc., 1967.

Hanslovsky, Glenda, Sue Moyer and Helen Wagner, *Report of Team Teaching Pilot Program* (Unpublished), East Lansing Public Schools, 1967.

Poles, Nicholas, *The Dynamics of Team Teaching,* Dubuque, Iowa: W. C. Brown Company, 1965.

Shaplin, Judson T., and Henry F. Olds, Jr., *Team Teaching,* New York, Evanston and London: Harper and Row, 1964.

PAMPHLETS

Davis, Harold S., *How to Organize an Effective Team Teaching Program,* Successful School Management Series, Englewood, Cliffs, New Jersey: Prentice-Hall, Inc., 1966.

ARTICLES

Marchak, John P., "Does Team Teaching Pay Off?", *Everyweek,* Washington, D.C.: Civic Education Service, Inc., January, 1968.

91

Spense, Marilyn, "Problems Inherent in Team Teaching", *Civic Leader*, Washington, D.C.: Civic Education Service, Inc., January, 1966.

Georgiades, William, "Team Teaching: A New Star Not a Meteor", *N.E.A. Journal:* April, 1967.

Fraenkel, Jack R., "Team Teaching: A Note of Caution is in Order", *N.E.A. Journal:* April, 1967.

McMillan, Gene and Evelyn Stryker, "How to Survive a Field Trip", *N.E.A. Journal:* October, 1967, p. 58.

APPENDIX

INTERDISCIPLINARY LESSON PLAN

United Nations   Pictures, charts, flags around room

1. Introduction
   Tour (oral) of different cities, and what tourists would see, ending in New York City. Oral discussion.
2. Colored slides — tour of UN
   Interior:
   1. General Assembly chamber. Each country has 1 vote, can send up to 5 members. Chairman of the Secretariat. Pres. of UN from Afghanistan. 7 major commissions.
   2. Security Council chamber. 11 members, 5 permanent, 6 elected for varying periods of time.
   3. Economic and Social Council chamber. 18 members. Discusses health, education, arts, international cooperation in general.
   4. Trusteeship chamber. Look after trust territories.
3. Brief history
   3.1 1945, end of World War II. No UN yet.
   3.2 Results of war: Poverty, destruction, disease
   A bomb had changed the world; U.S. dropped it on Japan
   Axis powers were Germany, Italy, Japan. 21 years later Germany still not admitted to UN.

3.3 UN Flag — polar projection of world, wrapped in olive branches.

3.4 *Junior Review* magazine passed out.

119 members of UN now, 51 members when it was founded. 3 more may be added during this session.

Discussion of UN peace-keeping role, preventing spread of many conflicts. Failure so far in Vietnam. China and North Vietnam not UN members, but could bring matter to UN attention anyway.

U Thant Secretariat Head, now is most important single UN diplomat.

Discussion of representation of China in UN — Red vs. Nationalist.

Indonesia walked out last year, has not petitioned for readmittance.

Money problems — France and Russia don't pay their share.

Racial problems — African nations sure to bring these in. Today majority of UN members from Africa and Asia, though most were from Europe when UN began.

Chart of UN.

3.5 Supporters of UN claim:

U.S. paying more than its share.

UNESCO, UNICEF, WHO have helped under-developed nations.

UN has helped keep wars from spreading.

UN provides a forum where world's nations can meet and discuss.

Security Council has 5 permanent members U.S., USSR, England, Nationalist China, and France.

Of 3 new nations entering UN this year, all 3 combined have less population than Detroit. But one of these has larger area than all of W. Europe.

Five official languages of UN, Chinese is one.

4. Group work, choose observer, secretary, and chairman, and debate the statement:
   A weak UN is better than no UN at all.

5. Twenty minute follow-up discussion.

INTERDISCIPLINARY
ASSIGNMENT I

Name_____

RESEARCH PROJECT

When you turn your project (report) in, make sure to include all of the following material. I recommend that you place the material in the following order:

1. Outline: this is a topic outline used to organize all your information before you wrote your paper.

2. Final copy of paper: in ink.

3. Bibliography: you should use the correct form for a bibliography entry and use the correct order.

4. The rough draft of your paper.

5. *All* of your research notes.

6. Bibliography of background reading.

Those students planning to do an oral presentation instead of a written report, will hand in all of the above material *except:*

1. The final copy of a paper.

2. The rough draft of a paper.

In place of these two items, note cards (3 x 5 cards) will be handed in — in outline form (Topic) — from which the speech will be given.

If you plan to give an oral report, see me to schedule a time for your speech.

INTERDISCIPLINARY ASSIGNMENT II

MAJOR TEAM ASSIGNMENT

Purpose: To demonstrate your ability to obtain information from a variety of sources, to test your skills in outlining, sentence and paragraph structure, expression, chronological development, and the making of a bibliography, and to offer you an opportunity to integrate your learnings of three disciplines into one unified project.

Content: Select some subject of interest to you. Examples: firearms, medicine, status of the Indians, punishment, photography, folk heroes, art, cowboys and cattle raising, National Parks, outstanding families and their contributions, etc. Trace the growth and development of this subject *in America* from its beginning to *the present.*

Form: Basically this is to be a written report, 3–5 pages in length (which means it will have to be tightly organized and concise with accurate word usage). It will include in the following order:

Title page (name of the subject covered and your name)

A topic outline

Body of the paper

Bibliography (at least three sources, including one periodical)

First draft (remember: a first draft is not just a pencil copy of the final paper).

Final copy must be written in ink.

Grading: Grade will be based on the following scale:

Title page   3
Outline   20
Body   60
Bibliography 15
First draft   2

Extra Credit: You may supply any illustrations, demonstrations, objects, etc., to illustrate your subject. Extra credit will be given for the quality and appropriateness of these additions (not for the quantity alone).

Deadlines: Introduction of the project
Last day to select subject
Final check of first draft*
Written reports due
Special presentations of outstanding reports

*I will go over your first draft with you in class as soon as you complete it. All first drafts must be checked by_____.

Note: Feel free to explore any topic of interest to you, but be sure it is of interest to *you*.

INTERDISCIPLINARY ASSIGNMENT III

TEAM ASSIGNMENT FOR STUDENT (on a trip with his family for six weeks)

You will make an intensive and extensive study of the state of Florida, to cover points listed below. Your report can be organized any way you choose, and may contain original illustrations if you like. It will need a complete bibliography, a rough draft, and an outline, all made properly. You may use standard encyclopedias *only* for background reading. You will need to read "The Yearling" by Marjorie Kinnan Rawlings, a Floridian; other books by her ("South Moon Under", "Cross Creek") are suggested readings. Other sources we suggest you contact for information are: local branch of the U.S. Geological Survey for maps of all kinds; local historical society for pamphlets and local color; Florida Chamber of Commerce; local library, which can borrow materials from other libraries for you; pamphlets for sale in tourist towns with local legends and points of interest. You will do some of your research in the field. You may want to contact some of these places immediately or to take some books and materials with you which you know won't be available in Florida.

Your finished report should be in correct English, in ink, with attention to spelling, punctuation, sentence structure and paragraphs.

Points to cover in report

1. Geology of Florida
   1.1 Geologic age, when it was formed and how.
       What was going on in the rest of the U.S. then?
   1.2 Current geologic make-up.
       Strata of its formations.

Types of soil, rocks, shells; special emphasis on unique qualities Florida has.
Variations from east to west coast.
1.3   Growth or shrinking of Florida peninsula.
Predictions for its future, and reasons for them.
1.4   A map of Florida showing elevation.
2.   Ecology of Florida
2.1   Representative plants and animals, in lists.
Pick 2 or 3 plants which are unique to Florida and give some information about them. Be sure to include the reasons why they occur only in Florida. Do the same for 3 animals.
2.2   Pick 2 representative communities of living things, such as the seashore, the Everglades, a cypress swamp, sand dunes, etc., which you can reach easily. Make sketches (to include in the report) of the plants and animals living in each, with their names and habits. Include whatever facts you can find about *why* those plants and animals live together. You may find a food relationship, or a chemical one, or protection, etc. Compare and contrast the 2 communities, after you have collected your information.
3.   History of Florida
Trace the story of the control of Florida by different nations until it was *finally* ceded to the U.S. Include the way each country obtained this territory; how long they kept it; changes during their possession; and how they lost it.

INTERDISCIPLINARY ASSIGNMENT IV

Name_____

Team Assignments

1. Write a short story about fictitious people living in the Revolutionary period. You can make up both people and events, or use real events and made-up people, as in "Johnny Tremain". The story will get 2 grades, one for English (punctuate, indent paragraphs, etc.) and one for science. The science grade will be based on how well you follow directions and how careful you are to have your characters use and know only what was available and known then. If your hero leaps into a sports car and speeds off, his creator is out of luck. Length: between one and two sides, handwritten. Write your finished story in ink, and staple your rough draft to the story.

2. From the list of principles of chemistry in your notebooks give for each principle listed below, by page and letter, two everyday applications. (See example below.) You can figure them out, or use your text or any other printed matter for help. In your work, identify each principle so I can grade it.

Example:

Principle: Bleach reacts with colors to form colorless compounds.

Applications: (1) The number of blonds increases faster than the birth rate of blonds.
(2) Bleach splashed on colored clothes leaves white spots.

Due:_____

3. Pick *any one* of the following, and write two informative paragraphs telling the importance of:

101

(a) Pasteur's discoveries about anthrax.
(b) The use of ether as an anesthetic.
(c) Henry Ford's pioneering in car manufacture.
(d) Marconi's invention using crystal sets.
(e) Watt's improvements in steam pumps.
(f) Fermi's atomic pile.
(g) The water wheel.
(h) Photosynthesis.
(i) ATP (adenosine triphosphate).
(j) Jenner's successful cowpox vaccination for prevention of smallpox.

Upper limit of length: one side of a page. Don't be tempted to waste space describing the person or substance or event. The assignment is to tell why your choice was *important,* and to whom.

Due:_____

SMALL-GROUP DISCUSSION GUIDE

Select a leader; a recorder; and an observer in each group:

— The leader is to ask questions and guide the discussion; in addition to reporting the conclusions to the total group.

— The recorder is to write down the points brought out in the discussion.

— The observer is to list the name of each member of the group and record the number of times he participates. The observer is also to rate each member's contribution.

Questions for Discussion:

1. Did young people have more of chance to be courageous and independent in Colonial Times, than they do now?

2. How do your opportunities to participate in important events compare with Johnny Tremain's opportunities?

OBSERVER'S SHEET

Group Number_____

Group Members	Times They Talked	Value

Leader of the Group:

Recorder of the Group:

Observer of the Group:

ASSIGNMENT NOTEBOOK FORM

ASSIGNMENTS

_____Day_____Date

Indicate absence or tardiness below: Name	Assignment Checked for Make-Up

English	Science	Social Studies

SUMMARY OF ACTIVITIES SUITABLE FOR DIFFERENT-SIZED GROUPS

Activities	Total Group	Inter-mediate Group	Standard Class	Small Group	Independent Work
1. Discussions					
(a) Question and answer			X	X	X
(b) General, open forum	X	X	X		X
2. Giving directions	X	X	X		X
3. Lectures (presenting new material or analyzing)	X	X	X		
4. Audio-visual presentations	X	X	X		X
5. Homeroom					
(a) Student Congress minutes and announcements	X		X		
(b) Homeroom projects			X		
6. Testing	X	X	X		X
7. Laboratory (science)			X	X	X
8. Supervised study		X	X		
9. Field trips	X		X		
10. Remedial help			X	X	X
11. Review and interrelating of ideas	X	X	X	X	X
12. Library visits			X	X	X
13. Pretest reviews and posttest explanations	X	X	X		

INDIVIDUAL TEACHER'S SCHEDULE FOR ONE WEEK

	M	T	W	Th	F
	Homeroom				
8:30 – 12:30	Team Block				
12:30 – 1:30	Lunch				
1:30 – 2:20	Individual Planning				
2:20 – 3:10	Team Planning				

Schedules for individual teams will vary. However, in order to take advantage of the flexibility of the team organization, a block of uninterrupted time should be scheduled. The increased cooperative planning between teachers necessitates a team planning period and each teacher will, of course, continue to need an individual planning and preparation period.

POSSIBLE TIME USAGE FOR STUDENTS FOR ONE DAY—A

	E	SS	Sci	M
8:30 – 12:30	3 — 4		2	1
			1	2
	1 — 2		4	3
			3	4
	Large Group Presentation			
	Very Small Groups (6 – 8)			
	Panel Report to Total Team			

A. A schedule of this type allows for a variety of activities and for a variety of group sizes. The English and social studies teachers combine their groups for a longer period, perhaps to pursue library research. During the same day, the science and mathematics teachers are meeting smaller groups for a shorter period of time. The large group presentation might involve a film. Ideas gleaned from the film could be discussed in small groups. In turn, the ideas from the small group can be reported to the total team. Time periods would, of course, be determined by the team teachers. As a general rule, however, it is wise to remember: the larger the group, the shorter the time period should be.

POSSIBLE TIME USAGE FOR STUDENTS FOR ONE DAY—B

	E	SS	Sci	M
	Homeroom			
8:30 – 12:30	Total Team Activity			
	1	2	3	4
	2	1	4	3
	Open Lab			

B. Schedule B would be most effectively used for two consecutive days. On the second day groups 3 and 4 would have sections of English and social studies while groups 1 and 2 meet with the science and mathematics teachers. An ideal use for this type of schedule would be the introduction of a new unit of study. General instructions and materials could be issued to the total team. In follow-up sessions with the various teachers, discussions in depth could occur. The open lab furnishes a time for students to pursue directions most beneficial to them individually.

POSSIBLE TIME USAGE FOR STUDENTS FOR ONE DAY—C

	E	SS	Sci	M
8:30 – 12:30	1	2	3	4
	2	3	4	1
	3	4	1	2
	4	1	2	3

C. Under the team arrangement it is even possible to use a traditional arrangement for meeting classes. By using this example each teacher would meet each group for the same length of time.

WEEKLY SCHEDULE PLANS

Team _____   Week of _____   _____ Marking Period   _____ Week

Teacher: _____

M				
T				
W				
T				
F				

111

AUDIO-VISUAL SUPPLY REQUEST FOR WEEK OF ____

Team ____

	Films and Equipment Needed	Room	Date	Teacher
M				
T				
W				
T				
F				

TEAM EVALUATION FORM USING OPEN-ENDED SENTENCES

Name (optional)_____

TEAM EVALUATION

1. The team is

2. If I were running the team

3. I wish

4. The kind of assignments I like best

5. The thing I've learned that helps me the most

6. In social studies I have learned

7. In science I have learned

8. In English I have learned

9. I'd like to study

10. During second semester could we

11. Being a good student would be easier for me if

12. I'll bet my teachers wish

13. I'd like to know why

TEAM ORGANIZATION
EVALUATION FORM

Name (optional)_____

TEAM ORGANIZATION

1. Things I liked about the team organization system:

   Things I didn't like about the team organizational system:

2. What should we be sure to tell next year's team kids at the very beginning to help make their year easier?

3. In your opinion, what changes would make a team operate more effectively?

PROGRAM

1. Name some skills you now feel sure of, that you lacked in September.

2. What subject matter have you learned this year that would let you carry on a meaningful discussion, argument, or debate with anyone?

3. What periodicals do you read regularly now? Check the ones you didn't read regularly last September.

TEACHER EVALUATION FORM

Please give your honest opinion and thought to answer the following questions:

*Teacher:*_____Name (optional)_____

1. What likable qualities or habits does this teacher have? Please name.

2. What undesirable quality or habit does this teacher have? Please name it below.

3. What are the most valuable things you think you have learned this year in this subject?

4. Please add any other comments on this sheet that indicate your opinion of this teacher.

OPEN HOUSE

Child's name——————————————————

Date of entry into school system———————————

Special talents and interests——————————

———————————————————————

Special health conditions————————————

Special concerns of parents—————————

———————————————————————

Contribution parent is willing to offer (slides, chaperon duty,

etc.)————————————————————

———————————————————————

PROGRESS REPORT FORM

_____
(date)

Dear_____,

Because of our joint concern about your child, _____
_____, I want to let you know that he (she) is meeting difficulties in my_____ class. I have checked below some of the reasons why this may be occurring. If you wish to contact me to discuss your child's progress, please call the school office and make an appointment.

Please sign this form and return it to me at your earliest convenience. Thank you.

Sincerely yours,

_____
(teacher)

_____ Possible causes of difficulty _____

_____ Failure to prepare daily assignments

_____ Frequent absences

_____ Poor performance on tests

_____ Reading problems

_____ Failure to make up missed work

_____ Inattention in class

_____ Work carelessly or hastily done

_____ Difficulty with self-control

118